C RE
'D   IN
READING RG1 4H
'7 5060

Reading College

K1002074

Delivering digital services

A handbook for public libraries
and learning centres

Delivering digital services

A handbook for public libraries
and learning centres

David McMenemy and Alan Poulter

facet publishing

© David McMenemy and Alan Poulter 2005

Published by
Facet Publishing
7 Ridgmount Street
London WC1E 7AE

Facet Publishing is wholly owned by CILIP: the Chartered Institute of Library and Information Professionals.

David McMenemy and Alan Poulter have asserted their right under the Copyright, Designs and Patents Act, 1988 to be identified as authors of this work.

Except as otherwise permitted under the Copyright, Designs and Patents Act, 1988 this publication may only be reproduced, stored or transmitted in any form or by any means, with the prior permission of the publisher, or, in the case of reprographic reproduction, in accordance with the terms of a licence issued by The Copyright Licensing Agency. Enquiries concerning reproduction outside those terms should be sent to Facet Publishing, 7 Ridgmount Street, London WC1E 7AE.

First published 2005

LEARNING CENTRE'S
GEN
2004
09

025.
520285
MCM

British Library Cataloguing in Publication Data
A catalogue record for this book is available from the British Library.

ISBN 1-85604-510-2

Typeset in 10/14 pt Bergamo and Chantilly by Facet Publishing.
Printed and made in Great Britain by MPG Books Ltd, Bodmin, Cornwall.

Contents

List of contributors

Lead authors

David McMenemy is a Lecturer at the Department of Computer and Information Sciences, Strathclyde University. He was formerly Lifelong Learning Officer for Glasgow City Council, where he worked on the roll-out programme for the People's Network. Other previous experience includes work on two large digitization programmes. His areas of expertise are computers and networks, user/staff training, management and marketing, and social inclusion. David is co-author of the *Library and Information Professional's Internet Companion* (Facet Publishing) with Alan Poulter and Debra Hiom.

Alan Poulter is a Lecturer at the Department of Computer and Information Sciences, Strathclyde University, where his areas of expertise are computers and networks, user and staff training, materials selection, and policy and legal issues. He runs training sessions on internet-related topics. Alan is co-author of the *Library and Information Professional's Internet Companion* (Facet Publishing) with Debra Hiom and David McMenemy.

Other contributors

Paul Anderson is Community Outreach Officer at the Scottish Parliament, Edinburgh. Paul was formerly Library Liaison Officer with the Scottish Parliament Information Services, where his role was to promote the use of Scottish Parliament publications within the public library network. Prior to this he worked in the public library sector.

Paul F. Burton is Senior Lecturer, Department of Computer and Information Sciences, Strathclyde University. Paul's areas of expertise include information policy and law, and ICTs in libraries. He has published widely on the issue of the ethics of technology.

Margaret Houston is Digital Network Manager (Greater Pollok), Scottish Enterprise, Glasgow. Margaret has over 20 years of experience in public libraries, including a long period as a young people's librarian as well as lifelong learning librarian. Her current duties include developing a community portal for the Pollok area of Glasgow.

Sandie King is Project Administrator, On-Track Project, Central College of Commerce, Glasgow. Sandie is a former Masters student in the Department of Computer and Information Sciences, Strathclyde University. Her research while there involved investigating the effectiveness of ICT training for public library staff.

Liz McGettigan is Information Services Manager, East Renfrewshire Council. Liz has over 20 years of experience in public libraries, and has been responsible for managing two prominent portal projects, Barrhead.com and Holocaust Memorial Day 2004.

Sara O'Loan is Research Officer, LGBT Scotland. Sara was formerly a Research Assistant in the Department of Computer and Information Sciences, Strathclyde University, where she worked on a research project investigating effective evaluation measures for the 21st-century public library.

Foreword

One of the UK Government's highest priorities is delivering better public services. The private sector operates in a British and global economy which is ruthlessly competitive. In this economy information is a marketable commodity and an increasingly valuable one. This work by David McMenemy, Alan Poulter and their colleagues is very timely. A handbook for libraries and community networks is not only useful, it is seriously important. If the library and information service is to survive, delivering digital services is central to what it has to do. If it takes up the challenge it will thrive.

I believe this work will be of particular value to those professionals whose formative education was in a time before the ICT revolution. Managing technology is now central to what we have to do. Creating content is central to how we help others do it and policy issues that relate to these are at the heart of our professional ethos. A generation ago community workers, including some community librarians, declared that in the desperate streets of many inner city areas 'Information is Power', which would enable those living in deprivation and poverty to take some power and responsibility to change their circumstances for the better. We now have a government committed to e-government for the better delivery of public services. We should never forget that e-government is about empowerment, about helping the socially and economically disadvantaged, about a just society; it is *not* about the development of technology for its own sake. If you want to do something about the increasing divide between the information rich and the information poor, not only in the UK, but in the global economy, then you need this book.

Professor J. D. Hendry
Councillor
Carlisle City Council
Former President of The Library Association

Introduction – Working in the 21st-century public library and learning centre

There can be few jobs that have been transformed as much as working in the public library has been in the past five years or so. A monumental change has occurred in the skills needed, and while staff have been trained to a high level in the use of information and communication technology (ICT) there remains a need for greater support in the area of ICT skills. As *Framework for the Future* stated: 'As the hardware of The People's Network is put in place, libraries, jointly and individually, will need to address how that infrastructure should be used, to maximise participation and spread the ability to use it creatively' (Great Britain. DCMS, 2003, 17).

The chapters in this book attempt to illuminate some of the key service issues public libraries and learning centres are facing. From the issue of ICT troubleshooting, to advocating electronic government services, to understanding portals and digitizing local content, at the core of the book is the goal to have the reader work creatively when using ICT in a public setting. In essence the hope of the authors is that the reader will move on from the more generic applications-based skills gained via training, into problem solving and the creation of resources.

Just why this acquisition of new skills is so vital to enhance service provision will be discussed in the chapters that follow. The core message of this book, however, is that public libraries can no longer remain static in terms of developing their ICT-based services to customers. The arrival of ICT-based services as a core stream of what public libraries do has had a revolutionary impact on the structures and staffing of the sector, but ironically the sector cannot afford any more revolutions. The institutions and the staff need to see their roles evolve as the technology evolves.

The wired library

It is often written that we are now living in the information society, and it is hard to dispute this fact. The problem with information is that there is a lot of it around. Every person on the planet has differing levels of information need and information literacy. Public libraries as a service that in theory must cater for all types of user are central to educating the population in information literacy. What cannot be allowed to happen is that we merely put the computers into the libraries throughout the country and allow the users to plod along. As a profession we need to be at the forefront of providing access to the technologies and the information, and this involves a larger set of skills than merely understanding how to use Microsoft Office.

This book then has several goals:

- to provide an overview of the policy issues involved in managing access to ICTs
- to enhance the reader's ICT skills knowledge from applications-based knowledge to problem solving and a more holistic knowledge of ICT and how it works
- to give the opportunity for the reader to expand their ICT knowledge even further into content creation.

As well as material from the two lead authors, contributions from knowledgeable practitioners have been added, which enhance the book greatly and provide case studies to support the key points made in the chapters. A full list of contributors is included at the beginning of the book, with biographical information about each person. We thank all of them for their help in developing this book.

Delivering Digital Services is split into three distinct sections. The first deals with policy and background issues relating to why ICTs have become so important in public libraries. This section also gives a thorough background to the legal and policy issues that arise in the daily work of libraries, such as copyright, acceptable use and filtering. In other words, knowledge front-line staff simply should not be without.

The second section moves into the area of building on existing ICT skills. The first chapter in this section discusses ICT skills from advanced web searching, to multimedia and understanding networks, to using Excel for effective survey evaluation. The final chapter in this section discusses how public library staff can place themselves at the centre stage of providing electronic government services to customers.

The final section is about more advanced ICT skills in the context of using ICT for content creation in the library. It discusses web page creation and design and XML, building simple portals for information sources, and digitization of local materials. All are issues that may be being developed at a central level in local authorities, but the skills delineated in this section involve using no more than standard Microsoft Office applications to achieve high quality effects.

The book is designed to be used flexibly by the reader. While reading in one sitting should prove beneficial, we hope equally that keeping the book on the shelf to dip into when planning creation of resources or to build up on knowledge would be equally fruitful. In addition, PowerPoint files for the activities covered in each chapter are available for download and use from the website (www.facetpublishing.co.uk/deliveringdigitalservices) accompanying the book, and are continually updated. These are free to use for staff training or for perhaps running classes for community groups or other customers. In addition, both lead authors are happy to receive feedback from readers or offer advice about how the PowerPoint files could be used in an organizational setting; feel free to get in touch with us.

We hope that the reader leaves the book with an enhanced ICT knowledge-base and a fearless attitude towards the deployment and development of ICT use in public libraries. The technologies are here to stay, and if used creatively can enhance customer enjoyment and service quality significantly. Finally, among the many goals we have for the book we hope it also reinforces the argument for ICT to be at the forefront of public library services now and in the future.

Reference

Great Britain. Department for Culture, Media and Sport (2003) *Framework for the Future: libraries, learning and information in the next decade*, London, DCMS.

Section 1

Policy and legal background

1

The role of the 21st-century public library

Sara O'Loan and David McMenemy

Introduction

In recent years, political emphasis on lifelong learning and social inclusion has had a significant impact on the public library sector in the UK. Public libraries have undertaken a diversification of service provision and rather than 'just' traditional book lending and reference services, they now support and provide resources for leisure, learning, information, advice, equity and citizenship. This chapter will focus on learning and the ways in which it can be promoted, supported and delivered in the public library, a place that has traditionally been seen as 'the working man's university' and the 'university of the street corner'. One of the public library's key concerns has always been with the promotion and enabling of learning for its users but the introduction of ICT technologies means that these learning opportunities can be delivered in new ways.

This chapter, therefore, has the following aims:

- to explain the policy backgrounds and connections between lifelong learning and social inclusion, and emphasize why understanding and supporting lifelong learning is so important in public libraries
- to discuss service extension and marketing in modern public libraries as a means of overcoming the barriers to lifelong learning
- to draw attention to some examples of ICT-based lifelong learning projects currently taking place.

What is lifelong learning?

The most commonly cited definition of lifelong learning is as follows: 'Lifelong learning is a deliberate progression throughout the life of an individual, where the initial acquisition of knowledge and skills is reviewed and upgraded continuously, to meet challenges set by an ever-changing society' (Brophy, Fisher and Craven, 1998).

Lifelong learning is seen to be qualitatively different from the traditionally structured learning that takes place in schools and higher education establishments. It is more informal in nature, can be picked up and completed at leisure and is learner-centred in that it can be engaged with in whichever way the learner desires. It focuses on the development of skills rather than the attainment of knowledge for knowledge's sake and is often delivered in a group setting. Crucially, conventional education is exclusive in nature, as progress requires prior qualifications; lifelong learning does not rely solely on qualification attainment. Table 1.1 is taken from the report *Distributing the Library to the Learner*, and helps to illustrate these differences and others (Brophy, 1997).

Table 1.1 The differences between conventional education and lifelong learning

Conventional education	Lifelong learning
One-off, discrete courses	Continuous activities
Knowledge transmission	Skills transmission
Formal	Informal
Institutional	Dispersed
Timetabled teaching	Any time/any place learning
Structured courses	'Bitty' modules
Teacher driven	Student driven
For individuals	Group learning as a social activity
Exclusive	Inclusive and pervasive

And Hawkey discusses the greater aims of lifelong learning:

> . . . if learning is to be more than the transmission, receipt and assimilation of knowledge, then the programme for lifelong learning cannot simply comprise action replays of earlier pedagogic encounters. There is an alternative approach, with an emphasis on participation, democracy and decision making. Rather than sitting in the stands, or cheering from the touch-line, ICT will enable learners to acquire transferable skills and to play a full part in the game, according to their own rules.   (Hawkey, 2002, 5)

In 1998 the University for Industry (UfI) was established in England and Wales along with the Scottish University for Industry (SUfI) in Scotland. These organizations were created with the aim of using ICT and e-learning to enhance the employability of individuals and the productivity and competitiveness of organizations. They were promoted under the brand names Learndirect and Learndirect Scotland. A national network of learning centres was established, all offering certified ICT courses and support for learners in conjunction with a website and telephone helpline. Learndirect and Learndirect Scotland use ICT technologies to overcome barriers to lifelong learning such as lack of time, cost, lack of confidence and inconvenience. Its pledge to learners emphasizes choice, support and flexibility in learning: 'We will work closely with our partners to provide a safe, welcoming and supportive environment where you can make guided choices about what, how and when you learn' (Learndirect Scotland, 2005).

Lifelong learning has become a political talking point in recent years for a number of reasons. In Scotland, the 1998 consultation paper from the Scottish Executive, *Opportunity Scotland: a paper on lifelong learning* (1998) stated that all Scottish citizens would have access to learning at any stage of their lives by 2002. Government publications such as these stress the importance of lifelong learning as a tool for the personal fulfilment of disadvantaged groups, but the constant upgrading of skills and knowledge is also seen as necessary for the wider economic and social development of society. The Scottish Executive's lifelong learning strategy (Scottish Executive, 2003) set the following goals:

(1) A Scotland where people have the confidence, enterprise, knowledge, creativity and skills they need to participate in economic, social and civic life.
(2) A Scotland where people demand and providers deliver a high quality learning experience.
(3) A Scotland where people's knowledge and skills are recognized, used and developed to best effect in their workplace.
(4) A Scotland where people are given the information, guidance and support they need to make effective learning decisions and transitions.
(5) A Scotland where people have the chance to learn, irrespective of their background or current personal circumstances.

The strategy identified the following benefits of lifelong learning for individuals, the economy and society:

Lifelong learning has an important and distinctive contribution to make to people's wellbeing, to a more inclusive society and to a vibrant and sustainable economy . . . . Lifelong learning policy in Scotland is about personal fulfilment and enterprise; employability and adaptability; active citizenship and social inclusion . . . [it]

encompasses the whole range of learning: formal and informal learning, workplace learning, and the skills, knowledge, attitudes and behaviours that people acquire in day-to-day experiences.

As a result of the European Year of Lifelong Learning in 1996, many publications, policies, projects and initiatives emerged, which continue to the present day. The European Commission recognized the changing way in which education is viewed and delivered, the knowledge that is available through modern technology, and the fact that unequal access can hinder social inclusion (Brophy, Fisher and Craven, 1998).

A wide range of learners can pursue lifelong learning: post-16 learners, adult learners, family learners and older learners. The activities and types of learning that come under the banner of lifelong learning are also wide and varied. For example, in Aberdeenshire public libraries, Adult Learners Week events in 2004 included internet taster sessions, 'Careers Scotland' workshops, CV tips and career change advice, international food tasting, stopping smoking advice, genealogy, an exhibition on different cultures in the local community, and careers and further education displays (*Aberdeen Evening Express*, 2004). Other public library lifelong learning opportunities can include sign language classes, book groups, creative writing programmes, basic adult literacy and numeracy courses, and classes for asylum seekers. The wide range of areas that lifelong learning covers are clear and with the introduction of ICT technologies and the increased government funding that this has attracted, many of these opportunities can be placed and delivered online.

In summary, then, lifelong learning is a continuous process of gaining and improving on a wide range of skills and knowledge. It can be embarked on in any stage of life, in a number of locations and is distinct in its flexible nature. Public libraries have always been places in which users could pursue learning and self-development; ICT-based or e-learning is simply a new way in which this can be facilitated and delivered. The main challenge now for library staff is to ensure that support and advice are accessible where and when it is needed.

Social inclusion in public libraries: bridging the digital divide

Recent emphasis on all things digital has brought about phrases such as 'digital divide' and the 'information divide' peopled by the 'information rich' and 'information poor', as a consequence of the all-new 'information society' or 'knowledge economy'. It has been suggested that new technologies have opened up new ways of communicating, living and working. Academic theory can be divided into roughly two camps: those who believe that there has been a decisive break with the past and a shift to a new societal structure, and those who state the case for continuity, arguing that information has always been a vital part of society and that the rise of ICT is just its current manifestation (Webster, 2002, 273). However, it is difficult to deny that new technologies have affected the ways in which we live and work – asynchronous communication through emails and SMS, video-conferencing, blogging, mp3 downloads and e-government are only a few examples. Most crucially, governments and supra-national bodies like the EU and the UN perceive the existence of the information society and are making it part of their political agendas. In this sense, the information society is very much a real phenomenon and must be treated as such by those who are expected to engage with it (Dearnley and Feather, 2001, 124).

It is supposed that a nation skilled in ICT encourages economic growth and enriches the lives of those educated in its ways. Governments in developed countries are therefore eager to use ICT to its full potential but while just over half of all households in the UK are connected to the internet, the rest stand on the other side of the digital divide. ICT know-how and PC ownership has a proven correlation with economic and cultural capital and, more often than not, shortage of ICT skills is a result of financial constraint. The fear is that a new information underclass is being created: those who are unable or unwilling to access the internet and become information literate will be unable to voice their opinions and concerns in the public domain. Although the interactivity of the web opens up a new and exciting public space it is not yet available to all. If knowledge is power then the ability to access information is paramount (McIntosh, 1999).

The government is trying to instil ICT skills in children from a young age and secondary schools are spending an increasing amount on ICT facilities and internet access. The average secondary school spent £65,000 on ICT in 2002, a third more than in 2001, and this figure is likely to increase each year (Liddle, 2003). Investment in lifelong learning in locations such as the public library and learning centre is an attempt to instil these skills in older citizens who have perhaps missed out on traditional learning opportunities. The insecure modern labour market means that jobs are no longer for life and constant reskilling and skills consolidation have become necessary. This is the case even for the ostensibly information-rich, given the currently qualification saturated job market. However, for those who have left school with no qualifications and are unemployed or in low-income employment, the need for skills and self-development is even greater. Engaging in lifelong learning may benefit the self-esteem of those concerned while also addressing the skills shortage in the UK workforce.

Lifelong learning and social inclusion are virtually inseparable in political terms and are key to both national and local government policy. The Scottish Executive's *Digital Inclusion Strategy* states that: 'A digitally-inclusive Scotland will ensure more equal, effective and beneficial access for all people to the digital technologies and web facilities that benefit them in their day-to-day lives' (2001b). Makin and Craven (1999) make the point that the public library service should rise to the challenges set by new government policies such as these given that they underpin education, enhance access to the world's storehouse of knowledge information and promote social inclusion by helping bridge the gap between those who are financially able to access information and those who are not.

Lifelong learning in the public library and learning centre: the People's Network

So how has the public library risen to this challenge? It is worthwhile, in this context, to provide a summary of the People's Network (PN) programme.

> Tomorrow's new library will be a key agent in enabling people of all ages to prosper in the information society – helping them acquire new skills for employment, use information creatively, and improve the quality of their lives. Libraries will play a central role in the University for Industry, in lifelong learning projects, and in support of any individual who undertakes self-development.
>
> (Library and Information Commission, 1997)

The 1997 report *New Library: the People's Network* (LIC, 1997) led to all UK public libraries being provided with PCs and internet access. This was completed on time and within budget in 2002. A key aim of the networked public library lay with education and lifelong learning. The report claimed that the public library was 'the natural place' for learning and skills development and that library staff were crucial in offering support and resources for people of all ages who were involved in formal or informal learning. Many public libraries have become learndirect-branded learning centres; in Glasgow the Real initiative aimed to turn Glasgow into Britain's first 'learning city' and learndirect scotland accredited learning centres were established in many of the city's public libraries and colleges.

Free access to PCs, the world wide web and online learning opportunities is designed to overcome the digital divide and provide ICT technologies to those who could not otherwise afford them. Through the public library, users gained access to the National Grid for Learning (a gateway to educational resources on the internet), access to previously unavailable specialist libraries, collections and exhibitions, and support in searching for and evaluating internet resources. Information and guidance on learning opportunities were made available along with online application facilities and links to information on grants, awards and finance for learning. The networked nature of the PN library meant that public library services moved outwith the physical confines of the library building and users could, for the first time, remotely access library resources and support.

By 2004 there were over 30,000 PCs available in public libraries in England and Wales, with an average of seven PCs per library (Brophy, 2004, 21). This is a transformation from the position of five years ago, and demonstrates real commitment to ICTs in libraries. There is evidence that use of these services is especially high in rural areas. In the Highlands, PCs are occupied for over 80% of opening hours and in one of the most rural libraries, Port William in Dumfries and Galloway, PCs are used 100% of the time available (Scottish Executive, 2004). Lifelong learning through ICT has become commonplace and this has resulted in a change of role for library staff. The target of March 2004 was set for all staff to complete their European Computer Driving Licence (ECDL) in order to be able to support learners on the new PCs.

Framework for the Future, the strategic framework for England's public library services launched in 2003, reiterates that libraries have a key role to play in the delivery of lifelong learning projects as part of the wider education and social inclusion agendas of the government: 'The Government's *Skills for Life* strategy aims to improve the literacy, language and numeracy skills of 1.5 million adults by 2007. Libraries are ideally placed to recognise and support people who might benefit from tuition' (Great Britain, DCMS, 2003).

In summary, then, lifelong learning and social inclusion strategies are a key feature of the modern political agenda, and engaging with ICT and overcoming the digital divide is seen as a key way of promoting these ideas and ensuring that they become an integral part of society. Lifelong learning, it is hoped, will result in a skilled workforce that is able to participate in the information society and achieve self fulfilment and development.

Barriers to lifelong learning: service extension and marketing in the modern public library

Public libraries are said to be ideal locations for learning as they provide a nonthreatening and inclusive atmosphere for many. In 1999, the Department of Culture, Media and Sport (DCMS) published *Libraries for All: public libraries and social inclusion*, a document that acknowledged the central role of the public library in social inclusion policy objectives. Train, Dalton and Elkin (2000) claim that the philosophy that underpins social inclusion – the right for every citizen to be included in society – is one that is familiar to a public library service which has always emphasized the importance of equity for all. This was most vigorously apparent in the late 1970s and early 1980s where outreach library work was strongly advocated and many public library staff undertook community librarianship with excluded groups.

However, this traditional assumption is questioned in *Open for All?* (Muddiman et al., 2000), which claims that, during its 150-year history, the public library service has relied on a voluntarist 'take it or leave it' approach, which has left many potential users out in the cold. Services certainly exist but there will be no, or only piecemeal and uncoordinated, efforts made to encourage inclusion and participation. As a result public libraries continued to be underused by excluded social groups, and they lack knowledge about the needs and views of excluded non-users. In addition, the public library service has often been guilty of paternalism, elitism and a bias towards white, English, middle-class values. The truth of the matter varies from library to library in the UK but, ultimately, it seems that the public library service has the capacity and the general ethos with which to encourage social inclusion, yet more effort must be made to target the groups most unlikely to use its resources.

> Public libraries provide a learning network that supports formal education but also extends far beyond it. Reading, literacy and learning are inextricably linked. The self-motivated learning that libraries promote is central to the creation of a lifelong learning culture in which people expect and want to learn throughout their lifetime.
>
> (Spacey and Goulding, 2004)

Although the PN report was somewhat evangelical, and despite the fact that its facilities have made lifelong learning more accessible for many, it is clear that barriers to lifelong learning still exist and ensure that many are left socially excluded. These barriers can be institutional, personal and social or be connected to one's perceptions and awareness of the public library (Muddiman et al., 2000). Some of these barriers are listed below:

- lack of time
- lack of confidence
- remote location
- negative experiences in formal learning environments
- negative perceptions of the public library or learning centre.

Governmental proclamations about the suitability of public libraries for the delivery of lifelong learning will not, in isolation, sway the perceptions that many hold about these libraries: that they are dank, dreary and silent places filled with stern, bookish staff members. This could not be further from the realities of the modern public library but in order to disband these ideas some work must be done by the public library service itself.

Of course, public libraries have always had a culture of learning, lifelong or otherwise: learning is to a large extent their raison d'etre. It is clear that public libraries currently offer a diverse range of services and they can play a large part in the development of lifelong learning and social inclusion initiatives. However, these services, along with the skills of library staff, may go unused if they remain stolidly within the four walls of the library building. Service extension – or outreach in its earlier incarnation – is crucial to target those groups who would be unlikely to visit the library and engage in lifelong learning. Some innovative ideas are included in the case studies section of this chapter. Train, Dalton and Elkin suggest that:

> The librarian should . . . reach out to the local communities, forging links and developing sustainable partnerships. In promoting a culture of inclusion, and at the same time celebrating the individuality of the library user, the librarian will maximise opportunities for all people. All library staff must be proud of the contribution they make to the inclusive society, and should learn to articulate this contribution to all.
>
> (Train, Dalton and Elkin, 2000)

Boasting about the skills and achievements of the public library service is a traditionally un-librarianish activity. This, unfortunately, can extend to silence regarding the resources and opportunities that exist within the library. It may be assumed that the public are already aware of these resources but a key role for librarians lies in promoting new products and services to both existing users and those who do not use the library (Hull, 2002). Interpersonal skills are crucial in the promotion and delivery of services. Many staff feared that they may become redundant following the onslaught of ICT in libraries: the converse is, of course, the case. Those people who are engaging in lifelong learning for the first time are likely to lack confidence and necessary skills: support from knowledgeable and competent library staff members is crucial to their success and development.

Traditional outreach or service extension involved work in the community with excluded groups: mobile libraries to the elderly, books brought to hospitals or to prisons without libraries. However, many public libraries now attempt outreach from within; in other words, to extend services without leaving the library.

In response to falling visitor figures and competition from bookshops some public library services have opted for the retail solution and have attempted to re-brand themselves, often removing the word 'library' from their names altogether. The most famous example of this can be found at the Idea Stores. These ultra-modern libraries are located in busy and accessible shopping areas and aim to combine lifelong learning and culture with the book lending and reference services normally associated with libraries. The Idea Store is explicitly linked with the lifelong learning and social inclusion agenda:

> . . . the new buildings will help to boost educational, training and job opportunities in Tower Hamlets enabling local people to do well in an increasingly competitive job market and generally raising local living standard . . . Imagine a place where skills and training advice is freely available and courses are offered in the same building. A place where you can learn informally at your own pace, mixing with other people learning all sorts of new skills.   (Tower Hamlets Borough Council, 2005)

Similarly, the Forest Gate branch of Newham Libraries has been combined with the local benefits office and is housed in a multipurpose building known simply as The Gate. David Murray of Newham Libraries states: 'the old model of stand-alone libraries, glorious icons to a vanished past, is not right for Newham, and it's a privilege to provide something that has real relevance to our community – all of our community' (*Library and Information Update*, 2004).

On a lower level, other older libraries have responded to the new culture of lifelong learning and modern retail-centred developments by introducing cyber-cafés and comfortable couches on which to browse through books and magazines. Whether this type of approach is a positive or negative development is a matter of opinion; however, the existence of these modern multipurpose centres demonstrates the extent to which lifelong learning and social inclusion have penetrated and influenced the development of the UK public library service.

Case studies: lifelong learning using ICT

This section will provide examples of recent ICT-based lifelong learning and service extension projects which have been delivered by public libraries.

CASE STUDY
North Lanarkshire's Community Learning Hub

(Bennet, 2004; North Lanarkshire Council Libraries and Information Service, 2004)

One example of a successful move into e-learning comes from North Lanarkshire Libraries and Information Service. North Lanarkshire has low levels of educational attainment and employment compared with the rest of the UK and high numbers of benefits claimants and lone parent families. A survey of the local community by the Libraries and Information Service identified a clear ICT skills gap in the area. The survey highlighted the demand for access to learning materials, training and support not only from local libraries and learning centres but also from other locations and at out-of-hours times.

The Community Learning Hub aims to improve ICT skills, promote social inclusion and increase employability in the Motherwell North Social Inclusion Partnership (SIP) area. It was funded by the Bill and Melinda Gates Foundation and the Scottish Executive Public Libraries Excellence Fund and consists of three main components:

E-learning website: LogintoLearn

It was intended that the website would both interest residents in lifelong learning and provide the resources with which to embark upon lifelong learning courses. The site includes materials to support qualifications such as the European Computer Driving Licence (ECDL), online tutorials, CV guidance, study tips and links to other learning agencies. Queries from remote learners are answered via a package called WebHelpLive, which provides real-time web-based support. In addition, access is available to online reference databases and e-books.

The success of LogintoLearn is clear. There were a total of 1.8 million hits to the site between April and December 2003 and between September and December 2003 several thousand learning packs were downloaded from the website, Excel being the most popular.

Outreach worker

Rather than waiting for the unlikely day on which typical non-users will come to libraries and learning centres to use unmarketed services, the outreach worker worked to deliver and raise awareness of lifelong learning opportunities to the residents of North Lanarkshire. Outreach was carried out in partnership with other lifelong learning agencies in the area to enable post-funding sustainability. As the libraries involved were SQA and ECDL approved the outreach worker could both support open learning and assist users in gaining recognized qualifications. Over one year, 125 learners enrolled in courses with ECDL being the most popular. Online courses and learning materials were downloaded from the LogintoLearn website.

Laptop loans scheme

This is an increasingly popular initiative and, in Scotland, West Dunbartonshire Libraries also provide laptops for loan. In North Lanarkshire, uptake was low as many of those who were offered the service were worried about the responsibility of taking responsibility for such expensive equipment. However, of those who took advantage of the scheme, 90% claimed that it had helped their progress and allowed them to practise new ICT skills.

Although funding is obviously the key issue when investigating the viability of any such initiative, the North Lanarkshire experience is an example of a public library project which understood the need for local ICT lifelong learning initiatives and attempted to surmount the barriers to lifelong learning which may be present in areas of social and economic deprivation.

Gosport Library is also located in an area of social and economic deprivation. Its experiences offer insight into a more low-budget marketing and lifelong learning project which provided high impact results.

CASE STUDY
Gosport Library: Change Your Life? A project for adult learners (Denyer, Gill and Turner, 2003)

The 'Change Your Life?' project had the following aims:

- to promote the library as a resource for lifelong learning
- to promote the services offered by the local information and advice worker
- to raise awareness of careers and education information.

Key to the project was collaboration with the Link2Learn Partnership, an organization funded by the Learning and Skills Council, which aims to help people into learning and work. Gosport Library also developed partnerships with local education providers. 'Change Your Life?' was to take place via a one-off event at the library with representatives from these partners and library staff available to answer questions and provide further sources of help.

Publicity

Promotion was undertaken outwith the library itself. Flyers and posters were distributed to partner organizations and information about the project and the public library in general was disseminated in doctor's surgeries, public notice boards, community centres and ferries. Full use was made of radio and newspaper publicity opportunities and information about the project was also posted on relevant local websites. Staff went informally to local businesses to spread the word and a stall was set up in the High Street:

> The aim was to get out into the community and challenge members of the public who were not library users to make the most of the event and look afresh at what the library service has to offer. Helium balloons and posters drew the attention of passers by and samples of books and leaflets on the theme of education and training were available for browsing.

Feedback and success

Examples of feedback from the visitors' book provided at the event included:

> Excellent, informative evening. I shall certainly return for more information, and thanks to you, I have enrolled on a computer course.

> I didn't know how comprehensive the library is today.

'Change Your Life?' was recognized nationally through the CILIP Public Relations and Publicity Awards and those involved felt that one of the many benefits of the project was staff development in organizing and promoting the event. In addition, as well as raising awareness about lifelong learning and ICT opportunities within the library it also helped to publicize the public library service as a whole.

The event undertaken at Gosport Library is not strictly an ICT-based lifelong learning project. However, it was included to highlight simple yet effective marketing strategies which can be carried out with a minimal budget. Although actual services were not being taken out of the library, news about lifelong learning opportunities was being publicized outwith the four walls and this is something that can only benefit the library as a whole.

Conclusion

Lifelong learning and social inclusion are important policy objectives for the current government. As the government-funded public library service is accordingly influenced by its policies, it cannot fail to be affected by these developments. However, engagement with lifelong learning and social inclusion initiatives is natural to the public library service in any case and it is crucially placed to support further developments; learning has always been one of the central activities for the public library and it has the capacity and ethos necessary for outreach, inclusion and accessibility for all.

ICT technologies represent a new and exciting way in which to deliver and encourage learning, and further suggestions of how to do this will be examined in the following chapters. Crucial to any ICT-based lifelong learning project is a commitment from library staff to encouraging learning and development in all users and a desire to provide the much-needed support for learners using library ICT resources. An extension of this commitment lies in appropriate marketing and service extension techniques. Learners will not beat down the doors to the library to use unmarketed resources and services; it is ultimately the responsibility of the public library service to raise awareness of these services and opportunities and promote lifelong learning to all groups in society.

References

Aberdeen Evening Express (2004) Adults Get a Chance to Book up Libraries, *Aberdeen Evening Express*, 11 May, 16.

Bennet, C. (2004) E-learning in Scotland: the North Lanarkshire experience, *New Library World*, **105** (11), 410–16.

Brophy, P. (1997) Distributing the Library to the Learner. In *Beyond the Beginning: the Global Digital Library: an international conference organised by UKOLN on behalf of JISC, CNI, BLRIC, CAUSE and CAUL*, 16th and 17th June 1997 at the Queen Elizabeth II Conference Centre, London, UK, www.cni.org/regconfs/1997/ukoln-content/repor~22.html [accessed 20 March 2005].

Brophy, P. (2004) *The People's Network: moving forward*, London, Museums, Libraries and Archives.

Brophy, P., Fisher, S. and Craven, J. (1998) *The Development of UK Academic Library Services in the context of Lifelong Learning: final report*, www.ukoln.ac.uk/services/elib/papers/tavistock/ukals/ukals.html [accessed 10 February 2005].

Dearnley, J. and Feather J. (2001) *The Wired World: an introduction to the theory and practice of the information society*, London, Library Association Publishing.

Denyer, J., Gill, A. and Turner, J. (2003) 'Change your life?': a project for adult learners run by Gosport Library, Hampshire. *New Library World*, **104** (1192), 354–60.

Great Britain. Department of Culture, Media and Sport (2003) *Framework for the Future: libraries, learning and information in the next decade*, www.culture.gov.uk/global/publications/archive_2003/framework_future.htm [accessed 31 January 2005].

Hawkey, R. (2002) The Lifelong Learning Game: season ticket or free transfer?, *Computers & Education*, **38**, 5–20.

Hull, B. (2002) Libraries, deliverers of lifelong learning – as strong as our weakest link, *68th IFLA Council and General Conference*, 18–24 August, Glasgow, www.ifla.org/VII/d2/inspel/02-3huba.pdf [accessed 17 February 2005].

Learndirect Scotland (2005) *About learndirect Scotland: our pledge*, www.learndirectscotland.com/about_us/pledge_to_learners/index.htm [accessed 5 February 2005].

Library and Information Commission (1997) *New Library: the People's Network*, www.ukoln.ac.uk/services/lic/newlibrary/ [accessed 15 February 2005].

Liddle, R. (2003) Secondary Pupils Struggle with the Internet, *Guardian*, 29 July, http://education.guardian.co.uk/schools/story/0,,1008190,00.html [accessed 25 January 2005].

Makin, L. and Craven, J. (1999) Changing Libraries: the impact of National Policy on UK library services, *Library Management*, **20** (8), 425–9.

McIntosh, N. (1999) The New Poor, *Guardian*, 22 July,
www.guardian.co.uk/analysis/story/0,3604,278694,00.html [accessed 15
February 2005].

Muddiman, D., Durrani, S., Dutch, M., Linley, R., Pateman, J. and Vincent, J.
(2000) *Open for All? The public library and social exclusion: Volume 1 – overview and
conclusions*,
http://66.102.9.104/search?q=cache:bd4HoGtTBncJ:www.mla.gov.uk/
documents/lic084.pdf+open+to+all+muddiman&hl=en&client=firefox-a
[accessed 17 February, 2005].

Murray, D. and Whittle, A. (2004) Through the Forest to the Gate, *Library and
Information Update*, **3** (2), (February), 28–31.

North Lanarkshire Council Libraries and Information Service (2004) *Community
Learning Hub Final Report: February 2004*,
www.slainte.org.uk/Peopnetw/Peopnetgatesreports.htm [accessed 29 January
2005].

Scottish Executive (1998) *Opportunity Scotland: a paper on lifelong learning*, Edinburgh,
The Stationery Office,
www.scotland.gov.uk/library/documents-w1/lllgp-00.htm [accessed 20 March
2005].

Scottish Executive (2001a) *Lifelong Learning: a summary review of Scottish Executive documents and action on lifelong learning over the past 2–3 years*,
www.scotland.gov.uk/library3/lifelong/life-00.asp [accessed 10 February 2005].

Scottish Executive (2001b) *Digital Inclusion Strategy: connecting Scotland's people*,
www.scotland.gov.uk/library3/enterprise/dics-00.asp [accessed 10 February
2005].

Scottish Executive (2003) *Life Through Learning: learning through life*,
www.scotland.gov.uk/library5/lifelong/llsm-00.asp [accessed 19 February 2005].

Scottish Executive (2004) *The National Grid for Learning Progress Report Three*,
www.scotland.gov.uk/library5/education/nglr3-00.asp [accessed 10 January
2005].

Spacey, R. and Goulding, A. (2004) Learner Support in UK Public Libraries, *Aslib
Proceedings: new information perspectives*, **56** (6), 344–55.

Tower Hamlets Borough Council (2005) *Idea Store*,
www.ideastore.co.uk/index/PID/14 [accessed 1 February 2005].

Train, B., Dalton, P. and Elkin, J. (2000) Embracing Inclusion: the critical role of
the library, *Library Management*, **21** (9), 483–90.

Webster, F. (2002) *Theories of the Information Society*, 2nd edn, New York,
Routledge.

2 Managing access: legal and policy issues of ICT use

David McMenemy and Paul F. Burton

Introduction

One of the challenges of managing library services in the digital era is the ever-changing nature of the legal and regulatory system. When dealing with the internet, there continues to be such a fundamental lack of understanding of its impact on wider society that it tends to be treated with equal doses of joyous wonder and rabid fear by many commentators. Each prominent incident of the negative aspects of the internet that reaches the public consciousness could lead to public authorities throughout the country panicking at the dangers they face in terms of liability as one of the main providers of access to the general public. Such challenges are regrettable, but unfortunately will continue to be part of the daily life of local authorities for the foreseeable future until society becomes comfortable with the nature of the internet and the inherent dangers that lie therein.

Yet managing ICTs is about more than merely the internet. Traditional concerns such as copyright, something librarians have been charged with protecting for decades, are even more of a concern in the digital age. The ability to digitize content and share it via e-mail across the world makes it a direct threat to the integrity of intellectual property rights. Considering libraries are in the rather unique position of acting as storehouses of intellectual property and offer the facilities to copy such materials, it makes them potentially liable if abuses are found to have taken place within libraries.

It is crucial then that public library staff are aware of all the issues involved when providing ICT access to the public. From acceptable use policies, to internet filtering, assistive technologies, to protection of intellectual property, to data protection, the public librarian needs to have a thorough grounding in issues that may be relatively new to them. This chapter, then, has the following aims:

- to provide a theoretical background to the legal and regulatory issues involved in managing ICTs
- to provide definitions of the main legal issues and solutions to these challenges.

The supporting website for the book points to further resources where information can be found on the topics discussed.

Why access to ICTs needs to be managed

Notwithstanding the logistical problems of managing access to PCs in public libraries, which pose many headaches for library staff with challenges such as booking systems and long queues, there are many reasons why access to ICT services needs to be managed appropriately. Resources are not infinite, as evidenced by the challenges presented to local authorities who are faced with the sustainability issues in replacing the infrastructure that was put in place from People's Network funding. In addition the risk of someone using a library computer to undertake a search for material that is illegal or inappropriate is quite high. There have been high profile cases where access to such material has caused a political scandal, an incident in Glasgow Libraries in 2001 being just one example where a reporter from a local newspaper turned up to a library asking why children could access pornographic sites on the internet (Nicoll, 2001).

Libraries have tried to address such controversy via two main methods. First, attempting to place the responsibility for the material accessed on the customer, via an acceptable use policy, and, second, by introducing filtering software to attempt to block the inappropriate sites. Both methods have their critics and could be deemed controversial.

Acceptable use policies

An acceptable use policy (AUP) is a document that a customer must sign and agree to before they are provided with access to the computer facilities. These agreements normally include a list of activities that are not permitted while using the computers, usually related to accessing pornography or chat rooms, and illegal materials such as copying copyright protected materials. Such documents tend to be used by organizations to pass some element of liability onto the customer when accessing internet services. The theory is that by signing an AUP you accept that any breach of the policy is your own responsibility and not that of the organization. Breaching the conditions of an AUP can have the following results:

- In an employment context breach of such polices can be used to discipline a staff member or to terminate employment.
- In a university, college or public library breaching an AUP can lead to withdrawal of the privilege of using the facilities.

In all cases of breach of a code the laws of the land may well take precedence over any sanction imposed by the organization. Accessing illegal materials could result in being charged by the police, especially if the materials involve child pornography.

It is very important that you are confident in your knowledge of what your organization's AUP contains. It may be the case that you do not agree with such a policy, and it is also the case that you may feel that many customers glibly sign such policies without reading them. Try to ensure that you make customers fully aware of what the policy contains and what they are agreeing to. It is the case for instance that some organizations may prohibit such use as internet shopping; not all policies are the same and you should ensure your customers are aware of this. In addition the responsibility to children in this area is of paramount importance. Many organizations demand that children are prohibited from accessing internet services unless the AUP is signed by a parent or guardian. Some libraries insist that the parent must come to the library with the child to complete the form, while others do not. There is, again, no overall policy in this regard that all adhere to. Ultimately parental responsibility needs to be stressed, and some kind of marketing needs to be undertaken in this context. Many parents are particularly ignorant about what the internet contains, but do not wish their children to miss out. Public libraries are well placed in this area to provide information, or perhaps even taster sessions on what parents need to know.

The policy of using AUPs should be backed up with a robust internet skills approach to ensure customers know just what the internet does and what is out there for them and their children. The notion of reader development is a strong professional domain aimed at enhancing the confidence and knowledge of customers in their reading choices; what is essentially needed for internet users is some kind of web-user development programme which does likewise.

While it may seem to be the safe attitude to take that once you have a signed

AUP for each customer then any breach is ultimately their responsibility, the role of a public library should encompass the promotion of internet literacy in users. Vigilance continues to be important, as accessing of inappropriate material may well offend other users who are visiting the library while it is being downloaded. The AUP is not a panacea for all problems, but it must be used robustly with confidence and full knowledge of its contents by all staff.

For those readers interested in a fuller discussion of the ethical issues relating to AUPs, Paul Sturges' *Public Internet Access in Libraries and Information Services* discusses the themes, and gives excellent advice on how to develop and implement an AUP (Sturges, 2002).

Internet filtering

Filtering of internet content is quite simply a form of censorship. It is an acceptable form of censorship for many organizations, but it is in the raw definition of the word, censorship. Indeed filtering is perhaps the most controversial of all management decisions that are made when it comes to providing internet access.

The basic dilemma faced by libraries that filter is the argument that it is one of the core responsibilities of the librarian to provide free and uncensored access to information. This is certainly true and neither the American Library Association (ALA) nor the Chartered Institute of Library and Information Professionals (CILIP) can be described as supporters of filtering. They do take a pragmatic approach, however, suggesting that in an ideal world we should never censor information we supply to customers, but acknowledge the unique dimension the internet offers for providing easy access to inappropriate material. This reflects the real world in that librarians may not wish to block access to information, but have to due to local authority policies at a central level.

The most common forms of filtering software use one or two approaches in blocking access:

- site blocking
- keyword blocking.

Some software programs use a combination of these approaches. Site blocking works on the basis that the software checks each internet transaction against a list of banned sites. If the software recognizes a site on the banned list it will not allow a computer to load up the pages from that site. This software needs constant updating, and it is normally the case that when buying the software the organization subscribes to a database of banned sites with their purchase. It is also possible with this software to add your own sites to the banned list, therefore there is an element of control from the organization itself.

Keyword blocking simply looks for offensive words in either the web address or the contents of the requested pages. If the software recognizes any offensive words it refuses access to the pages containing the words. The organization itself can specify the level of filtering necessary for both types of software.

Figure 2.1 shows a simple illustration of what happens when a customer accesses the internet in a public library with filtering installed. This model assumes that filtering is installed on the proxy server and not individual library computers, therefore the model may not be a representation that reflects the process in all library authorities.

When the computer requests a page, the request is only granted after the computer has been authenticated by the library's proxy server. This server may block access to the requested web page at this point if the URL requested is a known (and banned) inappropriate site. If the site is not known then the request will be made to the server hosting the web page. When the page is returned it will then

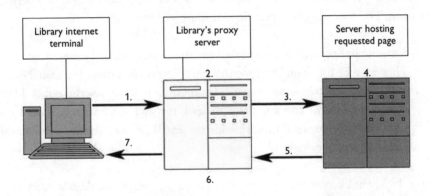

| Library internet terminal | Library's proxy server | Server hosting requested page |

1. Customer requests a web page via library computer. →	2. Library computer is authenticated by library's proxy server. If filtering software is installed it may block known inappropriate URLs at this point. →	3. Access is granted and request is made to the host server for stored page.
7. Page is delivered to library ← computer for viewing by customer.	6. Library's proxy server receives page and may analyse text of page for suitablility using filtering software. ←	4. Host server searches its files for page.
		5. Host server sends page if available, returns error if not.

Figure 2.1 A typical model for accessing a web page in a public library

undergo checking by the filtering software installed on the proxy server, although this time rather than the web address being assessed, it is the content of the page itself that is being checked for inappropriate words.

The main problems with internet filtering software are twofold:

- Installation of the software can lull an organization into a false sense of security.
- It can block access to legitimate content.

Many senior managers in organizations may not quite understand the limitations of filtering software. For instance, it is quite possible that, despite having filtering software in place, inappropriate sites could still load onto a protected computer. Filtering software is very much like virus checking software in that no matter how up to date it may be, it will not be up to date enough to provide 100% protection. Therefore the organization that assumes that it is protected against any inappropriate material being accessed is making a very dangerous assumption.

Blocking of legitimate content is more of a day to day concern for the public librarian. It is highly unlikely that all customers will ask staff for assistance when searching the internet, more so if the search they are conducting is of a personal nature. The following is a scenario that illustrates the potential dilemma:

A young person may be seeking information on sexually transmitted diseases. They may be too frightened to tell a parent, too embarrassed to visit a doctor without conducting some research on their own. They see the public library as an independent and safe place to look for such information. They run a search on the internet for information on sexual diseases, and the filtering software blocks the results.

It is highly unlikely in this scenario that the young person would ask a staff member to unblock such a site in order for them to access the material, despite the legitimacy of the content blocked. Other potential scenarios include the blocking of information on breast cancer, and information on sexual preferences. These are all obviously worst-case scenarios in terms of poor service to the customer, and with proper tweaking filtering software can get round them. It has to be said, however, that due to its role filtering software will always be designed to restrict rather than allow access. This core role, then, could be argued to be an anathema to the role of the public librarian. The ethical debate surrounding these matters threatens to roll on.

The Disability Discrimination Act

The 1995 Disability Discrimination Act transformed the rights of disabled people in the UK. At the heart of the Act was the need for organizations to examine how they operated with regards disabled people in three specific areas: 'For public libraries, the DDA has meant an examination of policies and procedures in a number of key areas including recruitment and selection, staff development and access to services, goods and facilities' (McCaskill and Goulding, 2001, 192).

Part III of the Act is the part that applies specifically to access to goods and services. Organizations were allowed a staged approach to making their services accessible. The milestones were:

- December 1996 – Since this date it has been unlawful to treat a disabled person less favourably than an abled person.
- October 1999 – Since this date service providers have had to ensure that they make any reasonable adjustments necessary to make their services accessible to disabled customers.
- Since 2004 organizations have been compelled to consider making any permanent changes necessary to make their services and premises accessible.

While making buildings physically accessible is an area that the majority of staff may not be involved in, providing access to ICTs is one where everyone can contribute through expanding their knowledge in the area. Using ICTs can be immensely problematic for people with disabilities. Computer keyboards and mice require a high level of dexterity, therefore anyone with motor impairment will find using these to be a major hurdle. Individuals with visual impairments may find it impossible to read a monitor and to take part in web communications as a result. Fortunately solutions exist for all of these issues, but the first priority for library staff is awareness of the potential problems and the potential solutions. The *My Computer My Way* website (Abilitynet, 2004) is an excellent first port of call for anyone interested in how a computer can be customized for people with disabilities.

Assistive technologies

Assistive technologies offer the opportunity to make previously inaccessible services accessible to disabled users. There are numerous types of assistive technologies related to several ICT uses, which are discussed below.

Pointing devices

Many disabled users have problems navigating a desktop using a traditional mouse. The most common solution to this problem is a tracker ball (see Figure 2.2), which is a large ball housed in a mechanism that allows the full hand to navigate the cursor on screen. This also means that users who may have arthritis can use this instead of a mouse to operate the desktop of the computer.

Alternative keyboards

Similarly to the mouse, many disabled users have difficulty in using a traditional keyboard. Alternatives exist that provide a solution to this problem. The key element in most alternative keyboards is larger keys (see Figure 2.3), but some use coloured keys as well as an alternative to the QWERTY key set up. This is normally achieved by simply putting the keys in standard alphabetical

Figure 2.2 Tracker ball
Reproduced by permission of www.assistivetechnologies.com/.

order, making the keys easier to find for someone not familiar with QWERTY (Figure 2.4).

Figure 2.3 QWERTY large keys
Reproduced by permission of www.assistivetechnologies.com/.

Software solutions

Visually impaired users may have difficulty reading what is on the screen and typing text on to the screen. Solutions exist for this, the most famous for screen reading software being JAWS. This narrates the contents of the screen to the user, even highlighting where an image appears and where a hyperlink appears on a page. The use of such software makes good web page design (see Chapter 5) all

Figure 2.4 ABC large keys coloured
Reproduced by permission of www.assistivetechnologies.com/.

the more vital, as sloppily captioned links or images will mean the software does not recognize the image or link for what it is. Speech recognition software can be used to allow the user to dictate to the computer and allow the dictation to be translated into text on the computer screen.

Costs

The challenge in the uptake of assistive technologies is in terms of the costs of the solutions. It is common to find only a handful of machines in a library equipped with the technologies necessary, both software and hardware driven. How provision of such technologies is accomplished is obviously a decision for local authorities to consider, but at the least it seems sensible that at least one tracking ball and large keyboard should be available in every public library in the UK.

Functions available in Windows XP

Remember too that Windows XP has some simple assistive functions built into the operating system that allows screen magnification, narration of some commands, and an on-screen keyboard. These can be accessed via **Start**, **Accessories**, **Accessibility** from the main menu. These are, it must be stressed, no substitute for the real thing, but they may offer you a pragmatic and free of charge solution to some accessibility problems you may encounter.

Copyright in the digital age

Copyright covers literary, musical, artistic, photographic, cinematographic works, maps and technical drawings and now also computer software and databases. It is often denoted in works by the symbol ©. Copyright is the right conferred by law to enable creators of information works (literary, musical, artistic, software, broadcasts and so on) to benefit from their work. Such copyright material constitutes the main investment and assets of information providers and they will wish to protect their intellectual property, as without such protection there is no incentive to innovate and produce new information products and services. In order to attract copyright protection a work need only be original or not a copy – it does not need to be novel. Copyright protection usually extends for 50–70 years beyond the life of the author.

In this increasingly global information based society the issue of copyright protection is one of increasing importance especially in respect of electronic information products and services. The internet poses particular challenges and is seen by some as one big copying machine. All copyrightable works are able to be digitized as computer technology can handle not just text, but sound, pictures and video in digital form. Once on the internet copying of these is effortless, costless, widespread and immediate. In the past copying intellectual products has been time consuming and reproduction was poor. That is now changed. With digital copying all copies are as good as the original in terms of quality. Furthermore the internet does not respect national borders.

The rapid growth of the internet and the rise in multimedia information processing pose new challenges for copyright protection and exacerbate the tensions between creators of copyright material and users. On the one hand creators of software and information services like databases wish recompense for their effort but users may argue that prices are so high they resort to copying. The counter argument from producers is often that they need to recoup expensive research and development costs and prices are high because piracy is rife.

The creation of multimedia products is another problematic area. Obtaining copyright permission on a large number of pictures, sounds, video clips and so on may not only be expensive but very time consuming. Some see this as a barrier to the development of new products. Some companies have bought up copyright to libraries of film, pictures and sounds as they recognize these information resources can be licensed for use in the future in a whole host of ways. However tools for the digital manipulation of pictures, sound and video pose a challenge – how much does something need to be altered before it is no longer a copy?

Software is easily available on the web to enable surfers to share their files across the internet, perhaps the most famous being Napster and increasingly frequently, Kazaa. While the popularity of such services is beyond doubt, they offer major challenges for information professionals both in terms of legal access to information, and in terms of managing the ICT infrastructure of their organization. It is highly likely that the computers in your library will be tightly controlled and limit such activities, but as customers begin to accept such services as standard, their concept of intellectual property protection can become less than robust. As Rupp and Smith have discussed:

> It has become a norm to download music off the Internet and transfer it onto compact discs (CD) without compensating the artist who created the music or the firms that created, packaged, promoted, and distributed the music materials. Few if any people think twice that they are breaking the law by making a copy of material to which they do not own the copyrights. Piracy . . . is rampant and routinely practiced throughout the world.   (Rupp and Smith, 2004, 103)

The new code of practice adopted by the Chartered Institute of Library and Information Professionals (CILIP) states that it is the ethical duty of a member to both: 'Defend the legitimate needs and interests of information users, while upholding the moral and legal rights of the creators and distributors of intellectual property' (CILIP, 2004).

And certainly it is difficult to argue that file sharing of copyrighted materials, despite the fashion towards this, should be supported by information professionals in this context.

There are more also more serious issues at stake in the copyright arena as content creators begin to assert their muscle. In March 2004 rights-holders began a high-profile campaign in Europe, following on from an earlier equally high-profile campaign in the USA, to bring to court individuals they claimed had offered thousands of copyrighted files free to be downloaded on the internet. The campaign targeted 247 people across continental Europe in countries where the record industry claimed that CD sales had fallen as a result of illegal sharing of music. Despite a recent study by two American researchers (Oberholzer and Strumpf, 2004) suggesting that music downloading was statistically insignificant in terms of its impact on CD sales, record companies are adamant that file sharing is impacting greatly on their income, and crucially are determined to do what they can about it via the legal system.

As an issue this will grow in importance, and there is always the danger that information organizations in the business of providing public access to the internet could become a target as customers who use public facilities to break copyright laws become a focus for rights-holders. In the context of internet service providers (ISPs) Conradi suggests that rigorous AUPs can shield the organization for much of the responsibility and pass the liability to the user where it techni-cally should belong. However, he acknowledges that there can never be a 100% guarantee that legal claims against the organization providing internet access would fail, should a rights holder decide to lodge such an action (Conradi, 2003, 289). Conradi also highlights the 2003 ruling against easyinternetcafe where it was ruled to be in breach of copyright law by allowing users to download music and burn the files onto CD on their premises. After a protracted legal dispute easyinternetcafe settled the case by paying the British Phonographic Industry £80,000 plus their legal fees of £130,000. This case potentially highlights the dangers in not being aware of what users are doing when burning material onto CD when using library computers. Unless you are 100% sure about your security, it can be difficult to know if a user is doing what eventually cost easyinternetcafe £210,000. The other issue to consider is that public libraries have many more potential service points that are potentially ripe for abuse than easyinternetcafe!

Copyright is essential for the protection of intellectual property and in this electronic age is becoming ever more important at both national and interna-tional level. Application of copyright has always imposed restrictions on the ser-vices libraries can offer their users. As increasingly electronic products and services comprise a larger part of collections and copyright law has been devel-oped to include these products and services, the rights and obligations of libraries in respect of copyright have become more complicated. Public libraries are guardians of intellectual property and in that respect will wish to fulfil this role effectively in order to facilitate the continued production of information and knowledge. On the other hand they are access points to information and knowl-edge and wish to provide their users with high quality services and the appropri-ate information and knowledge they require. The public library therefore has to balance the rights of users to access information and knowledge with the rights of information and knowledge providers to be recompensed for their intellectual effort.

Yet controversies relating to copyright threaten to grow in the future. As the next generation of users arrive in libraries, equipped with the download and file-share mentality, it is quite possible that their knowledge of and respect for intel-lectual property rights may not be evident. The role of the public librarian in this context is a vital one, not merely in the dual role of gatekeeper and provider, but also in that of teacher. Fuller discussions on copyright in libraries are available in either Norman (2004) or Cornish's (2004) works, both by Facet Publishing.

Licensing of electronic resources

Intellectual property also relates to CD-ROMs, and increasingly DVD-ROMs, many of which are available for use in public libraries. CD-ROMs can be anything from titles that support TV shows, such as *Changing Rooms* and *Bob the Builder*, to makeover software that allows you to profile yourself digitally with a new hair design, or reorganize your garden virtually.

One of the issues to guard against with such resources is the specific licence requirements. While copyright obviously guards against copying the material, an extra layer of legality is evident in many in terms of the stringency of their licence agreements. For instance, many CD-ROMs may allow a site licence for use, meaning that the material can be installed on all machines on site for no further charge. Others state that the software can only be installed on single machines; or others state that all machines can have the material installed, but only one user at a time can access.

Cambridge Information are a supplier of CD-ROMs to many libraries and offer advice on licensing issues. On their website they have a list of commonly asked questions, including:

- Can we upgrade standalone versions to network versions?
- Which titles are suitable for LANs and/or WANs?
- How do we calculate the number of concurrent/simultaneous users?
- Which titles can be cached?
- Which titles are NT network compatible?
- Which titles have paper licences (licence only which needs to be purchased in addition to the standalone software)?
- Which titles have full network versions (includes software and licence)? (Cambridge Information, 2005)

As can be seen, the purchase of CD-ROMs cannot be assumed to be as straightforward as that of traditional resources such as books. It is important when buying such materials that the librarian understands all limitations of use that the licence imposes. Suppliers should be able to offer advice on such issues, but if in doubt ask, and even more importantly ensure that all staff are knowledgeable about the licences of all CD-ROMs available for use in the library. For instance, it may be worth considering putting small advice notes either on each CD-ROM case, on the library management system, or indeed both. Erring on the side of caution would seem the sensible approach given the litigious nature of many content creators, besides which, as an information professional it is simply the right thing to do. Tempting as it may be, it is important not to be swayed if only one copy of a popular CD-ROM is available in the library and more than one person wishes to use it. The fact is that installing the CD-ROM onto each machine might enable all to use it simultaneously, may not actually allow you to do so. Essentially it is the analogue equivalent of photocopying a book to allow multiple users to borrow it.

Data protection – data privacy and safety online

Every day across the world people visit websites that record information about them. It is quite likely that the next time you are on duty in the library, members of the public could be visiting sites that require registration and demand they pass on personal details about themselves before access. It is also very likely that many of these people have little concept of their rights under law, and the uses to which this information may be being put. Thus it is important that public library staff are aware of the issues relating to data protection.

Data protection illustrates the inherent tensions which exist between the right of individuals to keep information about themselves private, and the requirements of companies and government to maintain information about individuals to facilitate commerce and the provision of services or to prevent crime.

Privacy concerns and the internet

Surveys of net users have often shown privacy on the internet to be a matter of great concern. Fears for the misuse of their personal information are an issue for net users and there is evident support for privacy laws to be enacted in the US. In particular the use of 'cookie' technology, which can potentially disclose personal information of unsuspecting web users is subject to criticism (Electronic Privacy Information Center, 1997).

While it is impossible, and undesirable, to be standing over customers' shoulders when they access websites, it is a good idea to have some kind of instructions for them on what to do if websites request information on them before they access. It is certainly true that not all sites who request information on their visitors are up to no good, but it is important that customers understand exactly what does happen when you pass on your details online. Very few of them will read the lengthy information provided by websites to state what they will do with your data, and even sites as straightforward as official football club sites require visitors to register with the site before they are allowed to view material.

A good idea may be to have posters strategically placed around the computer area of the library highlighting some of the issues. Some key points you may want to get over to your customers might be:

- Their personal data is potentially valuable; do not pass it on carelessly.
- If a site requires detailed information on them before they can access it, why is this?
- If they feel the request is unreasonable, complain to the site provider.

Conclusion

As can be seen in the discussion above, there are many legal and policy issues that impact on the use of ICTs in libraries and learning centres. Staff need to be made aware of these issues even before they assist their first customer, as ignorance in these areas is not only a recipe for poor service, it can also be potentially costly for a library where they are liable for any policy or legal breach.

References

Abilitynet (2004) *My Computer, My Way!*,
www.abilitynet.org.uk/myway/index.htm [accessed 5 February 2005].

Cambridge Information (2005) *Networking and Licensing*,
www.caminfo.co.uk/html/networking.html [accessed 5 February 2005].

CILIP (2004) *Ethical Principles and Code of Professional Practice for Library and Information Professionals*, www.cilip.org.uk/about/code.html [accessed 21 June 2004].

Conradi, M. (2003) Liability of an ISP for Allowing Access to File Sharing Networks, *Computer Law & Security Report*, **19** (4), 289–94.

Cornish, G. (2004) *Copyright: interpreting the law for libraries, archives and information services*, Fourth edn, London, Facet Publishing.

Disability Rights Commission (2002) *Disability Discrimination Act 1995 – Code of Practice: Rights of Access – Goods, Facilities, Services and Premises*, London, Stationery Office.

Electronic Privacy Information Center (1997) *Surfer Beware: personal privacy and the internet*, www.epic.org/reports/surfer-beware.html [accessed 5 February 2005].

McCaskill, K. and Goulding, A. (2001) English Public Library Services and the Disability Discrimination Act, *New Library World*, **102** (1165), 192–206.

Nicoll, V. (2001) Calls for City to Pull Plug on Internet Access as Watchdog System Fails: probe after kids use libraries to surf porn, *Evening Times*, 1 March, 6.

Norman, S. (2004) *Practical Copyright for Information Professionals: the CILIP handbook*, London, Facet Publishing.

Oberholzer, F. and Strumpf, K. (2004*) The Effect of File Sharing on Record Sales: an empirical analysis*, University of North Carolina, www.unc.edu/~cigar/papers/FileSharing_March2004.pdf [accessed 21 June 2004].

Rupp, W. T. and Smith, A. D. (2004) Exploring the Impacts of P2P Networks on the Entertainment Industry, *Information Management & Computer Security*, **12** (1), 102–16.

Sturges, P. (2002) *Public Internet Access in Libraries and Information Services*, London, Facet Publishing.

Section 2

Front-line issues in the 21st-century public library

3 The importance of building on ICT skills

Alan Poulter, David McMenemy and Sandie King

Information and communication technology (ICT) skills can be applied in a wide range of circumstances. It is one thing, for instance, to be able to use the types of computer packages found in the average office, such as word processors and e-mail programs. It is quite another to have sufficient knowledge about computers to allow a knowledgeable public service to take place and to assist others in using the same programs. This chapter has two main objectives:

- to discuss the background for the increased requirements in the areas of ICT skills for public library staff
- to provide a set of activities aimed at enhancing ICT skills.

The need for enhanced ICT skills competency

Asked by the UK government in early 1997 to provide a report on how public libraries can respond to the challenges presented by developments in ICTs, the Library and Information Commission (LIC) produced *New Library: the People's Network* in October 1997 (LIC, 1997). In this report the LIC provided a well constructed framework for the development of a public libraries' ICT network. Although the report was produced in 1997, initial research about which problems *New Library: the People's Network* should address began in late 1995. At this time, the LIC commissioned the UK Office for Library & Information Networking

(UKOLN) to survey all the local authorities in the UK in order to produce a report on the state of internet connectivity in public libraries. The resultant *Library and Information Commission Public Library Internet Survey* (Ormes and Dempsey, 1995) reported on the extent (or otherwise) of internet connectivity across all 167 UK local authorities.

Incorporating this survey, a further report (Ormes and McClure, 1996) looked at internet connectivity in public libraries in the UK and USA. This report found that in 1996 nearly 45% of US public libraries had internet access, whereas only 3% of UK public libraries had internet access. This translated into the fact that people in the USA had a 1 in 4 chance of walking into a public library and getting access to the internet, but in the UK this figure was only 1 in 100 (Ormes and McClure, 1996). The survey also highlighted the fact that people in both the USA and the UK had more access to the internet in a public library if they lived in larger urban areas, while those living in rural or remote areas were at a significant disadvantage in gaining access to the internet.

The LIC's 1997 report coincided with the explosion in use of the internet and other ICTs. Use of the internet had been steadily building throughout the 1980s and early 1990s, but the largest rise in the use of the internet occurred in the late 1990s, when the world wide web was well and truly born. However, with this proliferation of internet use came the first signs of what is now known as 'the digital divide'; that is, the ever increasing divide between those who have access to the internet and ICTs and those who do not. Prior to the LIC's report in 1997, the internet was just beginning to gain popularity and e-commerce was beginning to gain momentum. However, for many people the internet and even computers in general were alien concepts as the majority of those who did not have to use computers for work did not use them at all. Also, for many, the workplace was the only place where access to computers was a possibility and the boom in home computer use was yet to happen. Thus, for those who were not in further or higher education where computers and ICT were already somewhat of a mainstay, there was nowhere to access the internet and ICTs. The surge of internet cafés was also only in infancy, but even these were still considered by many to be the home of the proverbial computer geek and a place for people who already knew how to use computers.

As the previous chapter discussed, other reports of this time by the government placed further emphasis on the need for further and higher education institutions to play a key role in the delivery and sustainability of lifelong learning. Reports by the Department for Education and Employment that address these issues include: *Connecting the Learning* Society (1997), *Open for*

Learning, Open for Business (1998b), and *The Learning Age: a renaissance for new Britain* (1998a).

All of these reports, together with the government's response to *New Library*, explicitly placed public libraries as a key factor in the continuing education and lifelong learning of Britain's population. 'Education for many' and 'the public library is the poor man's university' were the popular ethos of New Labour and, armed with this endorsement, the LIC set out to produce clear guidelines for the implementation of its vision as set out in *New Library*. These guidelines were launched in the 1998 report by the LIC: *Building the New Library Network* (1998). Three key areas to be addressed were outlined in this report:

- network infrastructure
- training
- content creation.

Funding for these three key areas was to be provided by the Lottery's New Opportunities Fund (NOF), which gave £120 million for the installation of the New Library Network infrastructure and training and an additional £50 million to go towards content creation projects. In addition, £100 million was allocated to providing the New Library Network infrastructure, further supplemented by a donation of £2.6 million from the Bill and Melinda Gates Foundation, which went towards the purchase of ICT hardware for public libraries in areas of social deprivation. The £20 million allocated to training staff in ICT was to be supplemented by each local authority as it did not cover the costs of replacement staff while others were on training courses.

Staff training

The NOF guidelines stated that all library staff be trained in eight areas. Outcome 1 ensured that all staff attained the same level of basic competency in ICT and Outcomes 2–8 encompassed the use of ICT in the wider context of everyday library work. Traditionally, library staff have been trained on a 'need-to-know' basis, with initial training concerning basic library procedures, such as circulation, with additional training occurring as and when it is needed; for example, training in the use of a new catalogue or management system. With the advent of emergent ICTs, however, staff needed to be trained in the use of CD-ROMs, the internet, and other related products. For those libraries that provided internet access and ICT access prior to the People's Network, it meant that staff underwent ad-hoc training as and when they needed it and so staff within the same local authority or even the same public library could have had very different levels of ICT knowledge and expertise, depending on what ICTs they were exposed to. With the advent of the New Library Network however, all staff had the opportunity, and indeed the need, to attain the same basic level of ICT competence. This core level of competence was to be based around the European Computer Driving Licence (ECDL), a pre-existing training package built around seven core aspects of ICT. These core modules covered:

- basic concepts of IT
- using the computer and managing files
- word processing
- spreadsheets
- databases
- presentation
- information and communication (internet and e-mail).

The ECDL has now become a prerequisite for many public library jobs, with adverts for posts placing possession of an ECDL pass as a core competency for the post. Many authorities chose this as the default qualification for staff because it was a pre-existing package, but also because there was the opportunity to undertake the training online, which prevented the additional need of freeing up staff time for essential training. One prominent study of the People's Network training by Spacey (2003), presented at the 69th IFLA General Conference and Council in Berlin in 2003, evaluated the training methods used in 14 local authorities in England to teach staff about the internet. The majority of authorities surveyed in this study were using the ECDL to train staff for Outcome 1 as outlined by NOF.

The research found that although individuals obviously had personal preferences towards teaching methods, it could be (tentatively) concluded that online training in the public library could continue to grow in popularity. Another recent study has also highlighted the close link between staff attitudes to ICTs and training and the effectiveness of such training (Spacey, Goulding and Murray, 2003). This study again highlights the fact that individual staff have different preferences for training methods and that these preferences should be addressed in the ICT training staff receive if positive attitudes to change and ICTs are to be cultivated. ICT training is fundamental to the implementation of the People's Network and so it is important to realize the effect inappropriate or insufficient training could have on the staff that are to be using these technologies and indeed assisting others in their use.

Several other studies examining the necessity for library staff to embrace training are prominent in the literature. Such studies by Garrod (2001), Ondari-Okemwa (2000), and McNicol (2002) all highlight the need for library staff to have continued training in order to serve customers and fully integrate ICTs into the everyday routine of library work. Such integration would allow staff to use their new ICT skills regularly and become more familiar and comfortable with ICTs.

Building on the ICT basics – background to the activities

The activities that follow build on core skills in Microsoft Office applications and e-mailer and browser use gained through ECDL-based training by covering enhanced ICT skills from advanced web searching and multimedia up to and including troubleshooting. The activities assume you are running a PC with Windows XP. It is not enough to impart ICT skills to users, the focus must also be on ensuring that users know how to find and analyse information. As Garrod has stated: 'Learning in a networked environment requires users with IT and information skills in equal measure. Information skills include higher order cognitive skills, for example: evaluation, analysis and synthesis of materials' (Garrod, 2001, 30).

The activities are aimed at enhancing skills already in place in the reader, but some revision of material previously covered in other training will be inevitable. For more detailed coverage of internet-related topics see *The Library and Information Professional's Internet Companion* (Poulter, Hiom and McMenemy, 2005).

Advanced web searching

A search engine is a website that acts like a huge catalogue of the many pages available on the internet. If you are looking for information on a specific topic, but are unsure of the actual site where you find the information, you would normally visit a search engine to search for a site or sites that contain the piece of information you are looking for. There are many search engines on the internet, the more famous being Google, AltaVista and Lycos. Each search engine sends out a piece of software, called a robot or a spider or a crawler, to copy pages from the web into its searchable database. Not all pages are copied. The biggest search engine, currently Google, has over 2.5 billion pages (only) in its database! When you enter a search, Google will send you a list of all pages in its database with one or more of your search terms. The list is ranked so that pages with the most terms occurring most often come at the top, as these are the ones most likely to contain the information you want.

Activity 1

Assume we are interested in information on fuel emissions in Bristol. In your browser go to Google: www.google.co.uk.

   Type in the search term **fuel emissions** in the search box, then click Google Search. A new page will load with a series of results relevant to your search. Click on the links for the results on the first page. What is wrong with them?

   You should have found that most results were American. Try the search again on Google but this time underneath the search box you will find two options available for your search: Search the Web or Pages from the UK. Choose the option for searching pages from the UK, and then click on Google Search again.

   What does the 'I'm feeling lucky' option do?

Refining search queries

The material you found should have been much more relevant to the topic, as it is material from British websites. Assume you now want to further define your search by finding sites that mention fuel emissions in Bristol. To do this you add Bristol to your search terms so that they are now **fuel emissions Bristol**. By adding in search terms to refine what you are looking for, you can find more relevant sites for any research you are doing. Always try to be imaginative in your searching, the more refined your search term, the more quality hits you will get. If one set of terms finds nothing relevant try another set (e.g. use petrol fumes instead of fuel emissions).

   Another way of refining searches is to search for a specific phrase, like a person's name, or the name of an organization. You need to instruct the search engine that you are looking for the words as an exact phrase, and not as separate words mentioned on the same page. You do this on Google by enclosing the words in inverted commas. For instance, we may wish to search for information on the organization, The Scottish Environmental Protection Agency. In this case, our search term that we type into the search box would be '**Scottish Environmental Protection Agency**'.

Activity 2

Try looking for Bristol City Council's policy on fuel emissions.

Quality of information on the internet

One major problem of the internet is that information cannot always be relied on as being accurate. It is relatively easy to publish on the internet, and a search on a topic may result in hits that cover official sources of information as well as unofficial sources. It is important that you learn how to tell the difference. For instance, assume you were interested in finding out information on Glasgow. You may find information on various websites, but they may not all be official. The official website for Glasgow City Council is www.glasgow.gov.uk. How do we know this?

On the internet, computer names are made up of two parts, a host name and a domain name. A domain name is similar to the STD or area code in a telephone number. It tells you where the computer is, and what organization owns it. A host name is an identifying name for a computer within a domain, just like a telephone number identifies an individual in a particular area. Here are some typical examples:

www.strath.ac.uk
www.bbc.co.uk
www.glasgow.gov.uk

Domain names are normally in three parts and read right to left. The right hand part identifies the country of the domain. Most countries have a two-letter country code: uk for the United Kingdom, de for Germany, and so on. If there is no country code, then the United States is implied although there is a 'us' code which is occasionally seen.

To the left of the country code is a code showing organization type. In the UK domain these are:

ac   for academic
co   for private company
gov   for government
org   for non profit making organizations.

In domains for other countries, organization type codes may vary. For example, domains in the United States and Australia use 'edu' for an academic organization, while in most European countries 'ac' is used. The last element in a domain name is an abbreviated name for an organization. Thus Strathclyde University is abbreviated to 'strath'. Some organizations are recognizable, others are not.

The host name is the final element. It can be something mundane (like 'www' for the web server) or it can be something more memorable (like 'sloth'). There are exceptions to these conventions such as:

portico.bl.uk
pipex.net

In both the above, there is no organization type code.

The internet is difficult to use and understand primarily because the resources it contains have no physical presence for a user, other than on a computer screen. Host and domain names not only locate people and resources but can help the user to infer something more about new resources as they are discovered. Thus a UK television schedule provided by 'www.bbc.co.uk' (the BBC) ought to have more authority than one provided on 'sloth.cs.du.edu', a computer (host name 'sloth') located at the Department of Computer Studies at Denver University in the United States (a hypothetical example). This is a guiding principle, not a universal rule; there are some good sources of UK information located on computers in other countries. When working with the public, however, we need to be aware that they may not understand the nature of the internet and may assume information they find is legitimate. For instance there is great concern with issues such as Holocaust denial on the internet. Observers worry that children may access this material and assume it states the true nature of such atrocities.

Activity 3
Host and domain names are but one way of assessing quality on the internet. There is a good tutorial called The Internet Detective at: http://sosig.ac.uk/desire/internet-detective.html, which tries to help with this difficult topic. If you have time, register for the tutorial and work through it. Your progress is saved, so you can revisit the tutorial whenever you wish.

Types of search engine
Robot search engines
This type has already been seen as Google is a prime example. They are good for specific topics expressible by a rare combination of words (such as Chernobyl meltdown). However each robot engine may cover a slightly different subset of pages, thus not every page on the web will be indexed. Ranking can be distorted by index spamming (paid positioning of search results). Search facilities vary widely and change constantly and the help facilities explaining search options should be read.

Activity 4

Choose a complex search topic (i.e. one requiring at least three search terms), then search for this topic on the following robot search engines:

AltaVista
www.altavista.com

Ask Jeeves
www.ask.com/

AlltheWeb
www.alltheweb.com

WiseNut
www.wisenut.com/

You should find that each one produces a slightly different initial page of results, with pages being ranked differently and some pages not being found at all by certain engines. Save good pages as favourites.

Directory search engines

A web directory is a type of search engine created by people, not software. It is typically organized by an alphabetical index or a classification scheme. They contain links to far fewer pages than do robot search engines, but the links ideally will have been selected for quality. They may contain more than just links to pages – have reviews or ratings as well. They may also be keyword searchable.

They are browsable, so you can find topics difficult to word search for. In specific subject areas they can be very useful indeed. However they will not include everything, sometimes not even the best resources, and also may be out of date. Their quality depends on the selection process they use.

Activity 5

Using your complex search topic, search for this topic on the following directory search engines:

Yahoo!
www.yahoo.co.uk/

Open Directory
www.dmoz.org

About.com (collection of expert-compiled subject guides)
www.about.com

Resource Discovery Network (collection of academic subject guides)
www.rdn.ac.uk/

IMPORTANT: search by browsing only – by clicking on links. Do not use any search boxes. Was it easy or hard using browsing to find pages relevant for your search topic? Then try keyword searching. Save good pages as favourites.

Meta search engines

A meta search engine searches other search engines, usually many of them simultaneously. Typically keyword searchable, it has no database of pages of its own. Advantages can be that they save time and effort by searching many search engines at once. Their disadvantages are that they are unable to use any advanced searching features of the engines they use and they do not search all possible search engines!

Activity 6

Using your complex search topic, search for this topic on the following meta search engines:

Teoma
www.teoma.com/

ZapMeta
www.zapmeta.com/

How do they perform as against the single engines?

Specialist search engines

Specialist search engines simply list other search engines which may be worth searching. Some search engines listed are not general search engines and do not cover everything but will focus on particular topics, coverage or features. Some search engines listed may search data not on the web itself. This data not on web pages (but in linked databases and so on) is called the 'invisible web'. The invisible web is increasingly becoming the hot topic of the internet. Understanding exactly what it represents is very important for library and information professionals. Imagine for a moment you are using a subscription database such as Know UK, or a newspaper database such as LexisNexis. When you are a subscriber any searches within the databases look and feel like you are conducting a web search. This is however an illusion, you are searching a database whose contents are only viewable by the search facilities provided by the database company, and after subscription. This may seem relatively straightforward, yet there are many people who see the internet as a panacea and assume that searching for something on Google means exhausting all resources available. In the past, these users may have asked a librarian; in the 21st-century library they may feel they do not need to. This can be where specialist search engines prove an invaluable resource for the information seeker.

Some of the advantages of using specialist engines are that they may find a search engine dedicated to your topic. Also using the 'invisible web' may find more information in databases accessible via the web than in web pages. However, they may lead back to search engines already used or they may not lead to any appropriate search engines.

Activity 7

Using your complex search topic, search for this topic on the following specialist search engine (IMPORTANT: like directory engines one does not normally keyword search them but browse them for relevant engines which one then keyword searches):

Search Engine Guide
www.searchengineguide.com/

Invisible-Web.Net
www.invisible-web.net

CompletePlanet
www.completeplanet.com/

Profusion
www.profusion.com/

Did you manage to find new search engines which led to new resources?

Reference search engines

Many information questions boil down to simple topics. Reference sources (encyclopedias, directories, dictionaries, timetables, and so on) are ideal for answering simple questions. Not all questions can be answered by web pages. Books, journals, magazines and newspapers are traditional sources of information, some of which are searchable on the internet. Reference engines contain sources in these categories.

Activity 8

Using your complex search topic, search for this topic on the following reference search engine (IMPORTANT: like directory engines one does not normally keyword search them but browse them for relevant engines which one then keyword searches):

OneLook Dictionary Search
www.onelook.com/

LibrarySpot
www.libraryspot.com

Referencedesk.org
www.referencedesk.org/

Did you manage to find new information on your topic?

'People' search engines

'People' search engines can work in two ways: either they can lead to answers found in archived discussions or they allow questions to be put to experts who hopefully will respond.

Mailing lists are groups of people all interested in discussing a particular topic. Usenet newsgroups are conferences where people discuss particular topics. Searching past discussions of these can often reveal answers to questions. However, not all discussions are recorded or are easily searchable, especially for mailing lists.

If you cannot find the information you want, someone else may know the answer. Mailing lists, newsgroups and web forums are a good place to try asking your question, as long as it is on topic for the mailing list, newsgroup or forum. Search engines may just show the existence of a mailing list or they may enable the postings of that mailing list to be searched. However subscribing (signing onto) mailing lists can be tricky, as can viewing newsgroups.

IMPORTANT: never ask a question without first giving a detailed history of your search, or you run the risk of people thinking that you are being lazy!

Activity 9

Using your complex search topic, search for this topic on the following 'people' search engines (these are archives of discussions):

Google Groups (Usenet newsgroup postings)
http://groups.google.com/

BoardReader (web conference postings)
www.boardreader.com

DayPop (weblogs)
www.daypop.com/

The following are sources of mailing lists on which to ask questions (questions can also be used via Google Groups above on newsgroups):

National Academic Mailing List Service (addresses and postings of mailing lists)
www.jiscmail.ac.uk/

TILE.NET (addresses of mailing lists)
http://tile.net/

Topica (addresses of mailing lists)
www.topica.com/

If all other search engine types fail, it can be guaranteed that someone will know the answer you want, as long as you can find that someone!

Advanced search strategy

An advanced search strategy uses all of the preceding six types of search engine in a logical order, so as to maximize the chance of finding the information required in the minimal amount of time. Use at least one engine from each of the two main types (robot and directory) in order to get the benefits of both. Make sure you understand and exploit the search features each engine offers. Produce a favourites list of quality pages found. Then follow links from quality pages to find more quality pages. The six stages are:

1 Is the information you want available in a reliable source, such as a book, journal or reference work? Is it a simple question?
2 Search using a meta search engine (which searches many search engines at once). Good for quick searches.
3 Browse the web using a classified/alphabetical directory of hand-picked websites and/or guides. Good for general topics.
4 Do a keyword search of a software-created database of web pages. Be sure to make use of any advanced search facilities offered. Good for specific topics.
5 Browse search engines which list other search engines, looking for an appropriate specialized search engine that you have not used already. Some search engines may search data not on the web itself.
6 Finally try to find a mailing list or USENET newsgroup covering the subject area and after reading the FAQs (and searching any available archive) try asking your question, quoting sources already found.

Activity 10

Try out the suggested strategy. What do you think of it?

Multimedia

Multimedia is more and more becoming the means by which people are experiencing information. As internet bandwidth has increased it has become easier to pass around multimedia files, and many web services now rely on multimedia to attract visitors to their site. Look for example at the number of multimedia resources sites such as the BBC provide. It is possible on this site to watch clips from television programmes, as well as full news broadcasts. It is even possible on some websites to watch live football, or other broadcasts of events.

To comprehend multimedia images fully, sound and video need to be understood in detail, as well as associated technologies like file compression. Chapter 7 will see you using some of this knowledge to create more sophisticated digital files, but the following section explains the technical aspects to multimedia with some associated activities.

Images

A computer display projects various intensities of red, green and blue light onto each pixel (picture element) on a screen. Images are formed out of pixels. Bitmap (otherwise known as raster) image–file formats record images in terms of the pixels to display. They can be edited by altering the pixels directly with a bitmap editor. In Windows bitmap image files have the extension BMP.

Bitmap image formats tend to have large file sizes, making them unsuitable for sending over the internet, even in a broadband world. The two most common web images formats are the Graphics Interchange Format (GIF) and the Joint Photographic Experts Group (JPEG) file format. Both of these file types compromise the integrity of the image for the sake of compression, so they should not be used to store original artwork that is to be modified later. JPEG works very well for photographic images with gradual colour changes and no sharp edges. GIF works best for simple line images. GIF has a few unique features: it has limited transparency, so that one colour in an image's palette can be designated as transparent. An interlaced GIF, instead of being transmitted and displayed top–to–bottom like a normal image, is first displayed at its full size with a very low resolution, then at a higher resolution, until it finally attains a normal appearance. Also a GIF file can contain several images, along with a duration value for each one, to produce animation. For information on creating animated GIFs see: www.wdvl.com/ Multimedia/Animation/GIF/

The alternative to bitmap images are vector image files, which record images in terms of geometric shapes. These shapes are converted to bitmaps for display on the monitor. Vector images are easier to modify, because the components can be moved, resized, rotated or deleted independently. Macromedia's Flash is the closest thing to a standard vector format on the web. The W3C (www.w3.org/ TR/REC-png.html) has designed a true image format that can also be used on the web, the Portable Network Graphic (PNG). However it is not supported by most web browsers.

Activity 11

Go into Paint (available from the Start menu under Accessories). Use all the drawing tools and as many colours as possible to create a very colourful, busy image. Save your image as a BMP file.

Save the image as GIF and JPEG (JPG) files by using Save As. Do you notice any differences between the original image and the copies?

Load in your GIF image. Select (using the rectangular selection tool in the menu bar) a part of your image. Under the Image menu choose Stretch and double the size of this part of the image. Do not save your changed image to a file. Repeat this procedure. What do you notice about your image quality? Repeat this for your JPEG image. Which image was best at maintaining image quality when resizing? Repeat for both image formats except this time reduce image size 50% each time. Again note what happens to image quality.

Press the Print Screen (or PrtScn) key to copy the entire screen to the clipboard. Press Alt-Print Screen to copy only the active window. Go into Paint and paste a screen image of your desktop into it. Save the image as a GIF and view it in your browser.

Sound and video

As well as images sound and video files can be found on the internet. Most of the main robot search engines have options or advanced search features that search for sound and video files. Once you have found and downloaded to your computer a sound or video file, most common types can be played by Windows Media Player, which comes packaged with Windows.

You can create your own digital media. A computer is a capable digital-sound recording device. With an audio editing program as your recorder, you have the beginnings of a sound production studio. There is a multiplicity of sound file formats and software to create, edit or convert them. For information on the most important ones (MP3 and MIDI) see: http://directory.google.com/Top/Computers/Multimedia/Music_and_Audio/Audio_Formats/.

Unlike sound files, video files are much harder to create, edit and store on a computer. Chiefly this is because video files are huge files that take a lot of disk space. Video files will play in a small window in your computer screen, and they typically last only for a short while. As with sound files there are multiplicities of video file formats, see: http://directory.google.com/Top/Computers/Multimedia/Digital_Video/.

Activity 12

Try and find images, sound and video clips from your favourite TV series. To save a sound, video or image file simply right click on its link and choose Save [media] as. Save found files to you files folder and then double click on them. Appropriate viewer or player software (alerted by the file extension) should be started.

Streaming media

Sound and video files take a long time to download in their entirety and streaming them, that is sending just enough content to keep playing the sound or video, avoids this problem. Conventional sound and video files need to be converted into streamed format by special codecs or conversion routines. Special players for streamed files are also necessary. Apart from Microsoft, RealNetworks and Apple offer streamed formats. For free players for these formats see:

www.microsoft.com/windows/windowsmedia/9Series/GettingStarted/
home.asp
http://uk.real.com
www.apple.com/quicktime/

It is very likely that all three of these readers are installed on your library computer terminals. They pose incredible headaches for ICT support staff, as they are continuously updated, and many creators of digital media always like to use the latest version of a file format to create their files, rendering them unreadable on older versions of the software. There is no easy way around this particular headache for libraries other than to simplify the process of updating large numbers of terminals.

Activity 13

Go to each of the sites above and try to view some content of interest to you.

File compression

Note that often sound and video files (and sometimes large graphics files) are compressed, that means saved in a smaller amount of disk space than the original files actually need. To compress and de-compress files special software is needed, WinZip, Stuffit, WinRar and others. See: http://directory.google.com/Top/Computers/Software/Data_Compression/.

Activity 14

Go to: www.winzip.com/ and download the evaluation version of Winzip to your files folder. Once downloaded, double click on it to open it and install the application by following the onscreen prompts.

Downloading and installing software

As well as commercial software an enormous amount of shareware (software available for trial before purchase) and freeware (free software) is available via the internet. Many of these non-commercial packages are as good as their commercial (and more expensive) counterparts. Much downloadable software comes in the form of compressed files, which must be uncompressed (aka 'unpacked') before installation. Usually one of the uncompressed files in a software download is called 'setup' or 'install' and running (double clicking) on this file normally starts the installation process.

The following sites for shareware and freeware packages are recommended:

www.download.com
http://tucows.mirror.ac.uk/
www.mirror.ac.uk/

Activity 15

Browse the above sites looking for interesting packages to download. One tip is to look at their 'most popular' or 'most downloaded' lists to see what other people have been downloading.

Unpack any you find by double clicking on the compressed download and extract all files to your files folder. Or install it directly if it is uncompressed – downloads as an .exe or .com file. Then try and run it to see what it does by double clicking on the desktop or Run menu icon, or what looks to be the main program file (usually called [nameofprogram].com or .exe).

The computer desktop

Effective use of the desktop is essential to enable the smooth control and management of a PC. Once the desktop is mastered, then more advanced features can be investigated.

If you click on Start you get presented with a menu to access most of the important facilities on your computer. Choosing the Help and Support option enables you to find out about your computer and Windows itself. Choosing the Search option enables you to find files on your computer. Choosing the Settings option enables you to monitor and change what your computer can do, through the Control Panel, and also allows you to modify the Start menu itself. The Documents option shows you the files you last worked on and Programs leads to the software applications on your computer.

Activity 16

Click on Start and choose Help and Support. Try to find the answers to the following questions:

- What is the Clipbook Viewer? What can you use it for?
- How do you change the appearance of files in Windows Explorer from large to small icons? Why might you want to do this? What other view options are there?
- What key combination instantly deletes a file, bypassing the Recycle Bin? What is the Recycle Bin for?
- What is the Accessibility Wizard? What is a Wizard?
- How can you find out how much space is left on your hard drive?

Click on Start and choose Search. When searching, the '*' is a wild card and indicates any combination of characters (or none at all). Try to find the answers to the following questions:

- Find a file called 'notepad.exe' on your hard disk (normally the C drive).
- Find files and folders with 'windows' in their name on your hard disk.
- How many .wav sound files are there on your hard disk?
- What file(s) were most recently created on your hard disk?
- What is the largest file on your hard disk?

Click on Start and choose Settings then Control Panel. Choose Display. Try and change the settings of your background (aka wallpaper), the colours used on your desktop, and the screensaver used (and then change them back to what they should be!). Note that there are free collections of wallpapers, screensavers and 'themes' (linked desktop colours, backgrounds and screensavers) available on the internet if you want something different than those standard with Windows: see http://directory.google.com/Top/Computers/Software/Desktop_Customization/.

Try to find desktop items for your favourite television show.

You might like to look at and work out what they do (but do not change) the following in Control Panel: Accessibility Options, Folder Options, Fonts, Internet Options, Keyboard, Mouse, Network and Dial Up Connections, Printers, Regional Options and Sounds and Multimedia.

Shortcuts

Apart from the Task bar on the bottom of the screen, which shows what applications you have running, and possibly other icons on this bar which show available applications, the desktop is taken up with icons showing applications and possibly documents. These icons are important as you can add, remove and move them to suit your usage of them.

If you right click on an icon and choose Properties you will be able to see where on your computer the file for that application or document is stored. Desktop icons are known as 'shortcuts' to these applications or documents. Shortcuts are created by right clicking on a file in Windows Explorer and choosing Create Shortcut. This shortcut can then be copied and pasted or dragged onto the desktop.

Activity 17

Using Search from the Start menu find a file called calc.exe. Right click on that file and choose Create Shortcut. Say Yes to creating it on the desktop. You should see an icon for the Calculator on your desktop. Right click somewhere on the desktop background itself. Choose Arrange Icons and Auto-Arrange; this should remove the tick from against Auto-Arrange. Now click on and drag icons around the desktop. Turn back on Auto-Arrange and see what happens. Delete the desktop icon shortcut to the Calculator by dragging it to the Recycle Bin.

Installing and uninstalling hardware and software

It is very likely that you may not have permission to install or uninstall programs on your computers. If you are permitted, this may be restricted to CD-ROMs or DVDs that you have in stock, such as educational games and the like. The computers in your library or learning centre may be protected by either a hardware or software solution designed to prevent users from installing their own material. Such solutions include a software driven solution, Deep Freeze, and PC Bodyguard, a hardware driven solution. Essentially the goal for both is the same, they do not allow any tampering with the computer, either accidentally or deliberately, and they can only be updated by an authorized member of staff who is in possession of a password. Therefore while many of the activities discuss issues related to installing and uninstalling, please take time to read them even if you do not have such permissions, as the issues discussed are very important.

When you first get a computer it comes with enough software to enable its use and perform basic applications like word-processing. Over time new software might be added, and old software might be removed. The same might happen with hardware: for example a monitor screen might be replaced with one of a better quality.

New software typically installs from CD via a special 'install' routine. If this routine does not start when a CD is inserted, look for a file whose name starts with 'install' or 'setup' in the root directory of the CD. An example of a typical icon for such a file is shown in Figure 3.1.

Figure 3.1 A 'setup' icon

The 'exe' in the filename denotes an executable file, in other words a file that when activated launches a program on your computer. You must always be on your guard with regards to files with the extension 'exe', while most are legitimate program files, many can be malicious. A good rule of thumb is that such files received via e-mail, or from unknown discs, should not be installed on your computer.

Software applications also change over time. New versions appear regularly (many people think too often). An old version can have an 'update' released, which turns the old version into the newest one. Occasionally an application has a problem, which must be fixed by applying a 'patch', a software add-on which removes the problem. The best place to go to find updates and patches is the producer's website; for example for Microsoft Windows updates one would go to: http://v4.windowsupdate.microsoft.com/en/default.asp

When new hardware is added, your computer will need a 'driver', a piece of software that enables your computer to communicate with and use the new hardware. Adding new hardware should start the Add New Hardware Wizard (if not it can be started via the Control Panel), which at some point will ask for the location of the appropriate driver.

Typically updates and patches can be found by searching the software manufacturer's website, while drivers ought to be available from the site of the manufacturer of a piece of hardware. Updates and patches, when run, will install themselves.

Removing software is done by using Remove Programs, which is found in the Control Panel. Some software may have an uninstall option that is accessible via the Start menu. Please be sure never to uninstall a program unless you are absolutely sure you no longer need it, and ensure you follow the instructions that appear on the screen by the letter.

Activity 18

Try to find and download the following updates. Before downloading them, make sure you understand what the product is (software or hardware) that they are for:

• the Windows firmware update for a Kodak DX35000 digital camera

- the Windows XP driver for a D-LinkAir 11Mbps PC Card Wireless Adapter for Notebooks (DWL-650)
- the latest security update for Microsoft's Outlook Express.

Basic security

Computer security, apart from protecting the physical machine and any peripherals, involves the prevention of loss of data. Software can be replaced, reloaded if necessary from its original CD or re-purchased, but data cannot be so easily replaced.

The main way of protecting data is to back it up – make copies of it onto different media (floppy disks or CDs) or different machines or both. At least three copies stored at different locations should be kept. It is also sensible sometimes to keep previous versions of data: for example 'grandparent – parent – child' is a strategy for keeping three generations of data. Each time a new version of data is produced (a new 'child') the previous generations move up, the old 'grandparent' being discarded.

Data may contain personal or sensitive information. Data can be protected physically but a more secure way to hide it is to 'encrypt' it – scramble data so that only someone with the appropriate password to unscramble it can read it.

Note that deleted data is not completely irrecoverable. Using the standard file deletion tools in Windows (the Recycle Bin) removes only the name of the file from the file system. Its contents stay on disk and can be found and read by specialized disk-editing software. The solution is a special 'wipe' program, which deletes data by erasing it totally from a disk.

While a computer is connected to the internet it is theoretically possible for an intruder to use the internet to access that computer. A package that watches and blocks unauthorized external accesses to a machine (and watches outgoing connections) is called a 'firewall'.

Finally, also arriving from the outside (typically in e-mail attachments) 'worms', 'viruses' and 'trojans' are malicious pieces of software. Worms spread themselves and cause harm by using up system resources. Viruses spread themselves and have a 'payload', a harmful function, which is triggered by some event (such as a date). Trojans offer some useful function but also have hidden harmful effects. All these harmful programs can be detected by virus 'scanners', software that has a database of codes to identify each known worm, virus and trojan. While scanners are effective, since new worms, viruses and so on appear all the time, their database of identification codes needs to be constantly updated. It is good practice to have a virus scanner on each and every machine you have and to keep its database current (no more than a few weeks old).

Activity 19

One way of backing up data is to use one or more of the 'free space' services on the internet. Investigate these services via: http://directory.google.com/Top/ Computers/Internet/On_the_Web/Web_Applications/Virtual_Disk_Drives/ Directories/.

Sign up for a service and transfer a test data file there. Delete the original and then retrieve the backup.

Of course, storing files on a free service is not the best way to data security! For one thing files could be read in transit and while stored, so personal or private data is at risk. This risk is prevented by encryption: download and install a freeware package called Pretty Good Privacy (PGP): www.pgpi.org.

PGP can encrypt files and has a file wipe facility. It can also do a lot more than this, for example enable you to send e-mail securely and to add 'digital signatures' to content to show that you created that content. For more details see: www.pgpi.org/doc/overview/.

Zone Alarm is a firewall for Windows systems. It has a freeware version downloadable from: www.zonelabs.com/.

Download and install it. Be sure to read its documentation as setting up and using a firewall can be complex.

A collection of anti-virus scanners is available at: http://directory.google.com/ Top/Computers/Software/Shareware/Windows/Utilities/Anti-Virus/.

Some software and websites store on your machine unwanted and possibly dangerous tracking and remote access facilities without your knowledge. There are utilities which remove this 'spyware'. Spybot is recommended: www.safer-networking.org.

Finally, for an exhaustive security checker for any Windows system, it is recommended you download and install the Microsoft Baseline Security Advisor from: www.microsoft.com/technet/treeview/default.asp?url=/technet/security/tools/ Tools/mbsahome.asp.

Troubleshooting

Computer troubleshooting is especially hard to teach as a skill, as it is very difficult to replicate the types of scenarios you may see daily when managing numerous computers for the public. A confident approach to troubleshooting is desirable, however. It is often the case that a computer is deemed out of order, and thus out of use for the public, for the simplest and most fixable of reasons.

This will obviously have a knock-on effect, since reducing your capacity will reduce the quality of service. It is also off-putting as a customer to walk into a library where many of the computers have out of order signs over them. As well as being frustrating for staff and customer, it send out a negative image with regards service quality. Having the ability and confidence to troubleshoot minor issues is also a major confidence builder for staff.

Once a system is set up properly, new software and hardware are installed, updated and uninstalled properly, and security precautions are in place things should work smoothly. There are really only three potential sources of problems, assuming that virus infection has been prevented, which in most organizations should be as given. The potential problems, then, should fall under the following categories:

- a user changing settings by mistake (which solutions like Deep Freeze rule out)
- a hardware device or component failing
- a new piece of software or hardware conflicting with something on the existing system (for instance, running two virus scanners can cause problems as one can mistake the other's database of virus signatures for actual viruses). If a problem is noted immediately after changing something on a system then undo the change. If the problem goes then there is still the question of how to make the change to be investigated.

When a problem is seen, it is important not to do anything to try to fix it until the problem itself has been properly investigated. Simply changing things that look as though they might fix a problem can lead to more problems, exacerbating the original one remaining unsolved. The exact nature of the problem, especially any error messages, must be identified.

There are two places to look for information to solve problems. One is the site of the producer of a suspect piece of software or hardware. The other is conferences or mailing lists for areas related to the problem, as most problems are not unique: someone may have had that problem before. If a particular problem cannot be found in the archives (past discussions) of a conference or mailing list then the detailed description of the problem can be posted for others to help solve.

Once you have a potential fix the best way to apply it is to boot the affected machine in 'Safe Mode' by holding down the F5 key during booting. Safe Mode loads only a minimal set of drivers or software and is thus useful for changing settings and then rebooting into normal mode.

For help in problem–solving issues with Microsoft products see:

http://support.microsoft.com/
www.google.com/microsoft.html

Note that Google also offers specialized searches for Apple Macintosh, Unix and Linux information.

See the discussion earlier in this chapter on web searching for details of how to find newsgroups and mailing on particular topics, in this case computer trouble-shooting.

Activity 20

Try solving the following problems, but make sure you understand the nature of product/software that is involved, before attempting to solve the problem:

- **Problem 1**: I have a 4mm HP Sure Store 2000, and it has a DAT tape stuck in it. Any suggestions as to how to get it out?
- **Problem 2**: Is it possible to change the start-up/shutdown images for Windows 2000 as it was for Windows 9x?
- **Problem 3**: If I use an ISDN adapter to dial-up my ISP (Pipex) and run ipconfig /all (this is W2000) to view the WAN (PP/SLIP) interface details, I see the dynami-cally issued IP address and a MAC address. If I use the same adapter to dial up another ISP (e.g. Demon) ipconfig /all shows a different IP address (as expected) but shows the same MAC address. If I now use a modem to dial these ISPs I see the same MAC address. Where does this MAC address come from? Is it unique?
- **Problem 4**: Anyone know of a utility to print whole Windows Help files in a structured/formatted way? There seem to be an increasing number of programs with zero or minimal hardcopy manuals, but with respectable online (Windows) help, but I for one still prefer having a hardcopy manual to browse through.
- **Problem 5**: My children's (the games) PC has a peculiar problem. It tends to lock up periodically UNLESS I disable the LAN card. W98 system properties shows no conflicts, but the supplied diagnostics for the graphics card (creative 3DB GeForce 256 Pro agp) reports that it doesn't like to share IRQ 11 with the LAN card (but doesn't seem to mind sharing it with other devices). Disabling the LAN card solves the problem, but neither card wants to let me change their IRQ to an unused one. Any ideas?

- **Problem 6**: I recently needed to move my computer, which meant shutting down and unplugging everything at the back. Got it back together and everything seems to be working except that I have no sound. I shut down, checked that the speaker plug was firmly seated and booted up again. Still no sound (normally there would be a sound played when Win95 starts *up*). *Note: during this second boot up I noticed a message "Updating ESCD. Success."*

Setting up a secure network and internet connection

At the heart of modern computing is the network, be it a local area network (LAN) or a wide area network (WAN). The aim of this section is to introduce basic networking concepts and explain how to set up a LAN. Various configurations for a LAN are covered. Finally, setting up machines on the LAN for secure public access is dealt with.

Connecting a simple ethernet network

In 1973, at Xerox Corporation's Palo Alto Research Centre (PARC), researcher Bob Metcalfe designed and tested the first ethernet network, linking two devices, a printer and a PC. Since then ethernet has since become the most widely used local area network technology in the world.

Ethernet-connected devices all share a single cable. Once a device is attached to this cable, it has the ability to communicate with any other attached device. This allows the network to expand to accommodate new devices without requiring any modification to those devices already networked. Ethernet devices can have only a few hundred metres of cable between them, hence its use in local area networks only.

Ethernet is not a physical thing, but a protocol, which is simply networking jargon for the set of prompts and responses that devices on a network use to successfully communicate. Ethernet uses special terms: devices are known as 'nodes'. Nodes are connected by a cable, the 'medium', to form a 'segment'. Messages are known as 'frames' and must include addresses for source and destination devices. Since each node has a unique address, frames arriving at a node without that address as the destination are ignored.

To keep messaging simple, any frame is sent to all nodes on a segment. Without regulation, the medium would be flooded by frames and a simple mechanism, Carrier-Sense Multiple Access with Collision Detection (CSMA/CD), checks this potential cacophony. If a node wishes to send a frame it waits until there are no frames on the medium and then tries to send its frame. If a collision occurs, as another device also attempts to send a frame, it waits a randomly determined length of time before checking for inactivity and transmitting again.

How do nodes get unique addresses? These are known as Media Access Control (MAC) addresses. They are rather like ISBNs in that they are assigned to each device (like network cards, printers etc) on manufacture. Each company has a root code to which it adds a second incremental number for each individual device it makes. Devices will have their MAC address on them or on their packaging. Once installed a MAC address ought to be viewable using the 'driver' software supplied with a device. It is a good idea to keep a database listing devices against their MAC addresses, just in case!

Imagine you want to set up a simple ethernet network, what do you have to do? First, you need to buy a network card (also known as a network interface card or NIC) for each computer and install a card in each computer. Older cards run at a top speed of 10 megabytes of data per second, but newer cards handle 100 megabytes per second. The simplest network is formed by connecting the cards in two machines using a single twisted pair cable. However, most networks need to connect more than two computers so you should buy a device called a hub, and plug cables into each machine and then from each machine into the hub. The capacity of hubs to connect computers normally goes up in groups of four so buy a hub that has connect points for all the computers you have plus points for more.

One connection into the hub (normally the first one in its numbered sequence of connection points) will allow the computer connected to this point to run software supplied with the hub to set up the network. The set up involves essentially telling the hub the MAC address of each device connected to each connection point on the hub. Once this is done, the network infrastructure is operational! The last stage is to set-up whatever facilities the operating system you are using offers for file and printer sharing. You will then have a fully functional network.

Connecting to the internet

The first stage in connecting a network to the internet is to build your local network as outlined above. The internet does not use ethernet as its protocol but Transmission Control Protocol/Internet Protocol (TCP/IP). TCP/IP describes two sets of standards derived from a US defence project that became the basis for the Advance Research Projects Agency Network (ARPAnet) in 1969.

The internet protocol (IP) handles the addressing and routing of data. Data to be sent across the internet is split into several packets, which are routed as separate entities between the sender and the receiver. Thus each packet might take a completely different route (in terms of a part of network connections) between the sending and receiving computers. Packets might also arrive out of sequence and this must be handled by the IP protocol.

Central to the IP protocol are IP addresses, which uniquely identify each device connected to the internet. The format of an IP address is a binary number 32 digits long, which is represented as four decimal numbers (in the range 0 to 255) separated by dots, for example:

53.215.21.226

One further point needs to be made about IP addresses. They have another form more commonly known, called domain names, which are alphabetical equivalents of the numeric form (rather as an address is linked to its landline phone number). An example domain name of a computer connected to the internet might be library.biguniversity.ac.uk where:

uk gives the United Kingdom as a location
ac gives the type of the owning organization, in this case academic
biguniversity gives an abbreviated form of the name of the owning organization
library gives an identifier for the actual location of the computer.

The Domain Name System (DNS) performs an invisible, automatic translation between domain names and IP addresses. People find domain names easier to remember and use than IP addresses: however, it is the latter which are used in addressing and routing data in packets across the internet.

Finally, the role of the Transmission Control Protocol (TCP) is to check that the data in packets is not corrupted or lost when they move through the internet and that any packets that do not get through are resent.

So how is an internet connection set up? First, there is no need to remove the existing ethernet set up as this will be used by TCP/IP on the local network. Second, what is needed is a replacement for the local hub. The replacement is called a router and functions locally exactly as the hub – it enables ethernet connections between local machines but it also has an extra connection, which connects the router to the internet.

The nature of this extra connection is determined by your internet connection. The three types of internet connection suitable for network use are Integrated Services Digital Network (ISDN), Asychronous Digitial Services Line (ADSL) and cable. You need to buy a router that supports your internet connection type.

When the router is connected to the local machines, it will need MAC addresses for their NICs. But it will also need to allocate IP addresses to each local machine and it will also need an IP number for itself. There are two ways of allocating IP addresses for local machines. One way is to let the router do it automatically; in its control software will be an option to set up DHCP (Dynamic Host Configuration Protocol) so choose this option to avoid allocating IP addresses yourself. However, you can do this if you want and numbers in the range 192.168.0.1 to 192.168.0.255 are used. The router itself will need a number, typically 192.168.0.0. You may be asked for a subnet mask: this is a special number, usually 255.255.255.0, which means 'ignore the first three number in any IP address when routing data locally'. Since all local machines will have the same first three numbers this is sensible.

Finally you will need an IP number for the router to use as its internet address (192.168.0.0 is its local IP address). Your ISP will be able to give you the appropriate IP address and they will also give you the IP address(es) of their DNS servers. This information needs to be set up on your router. Once this is done, the router will be able to create an internet connection, and share that connection among the local machines that are connected to it.

Some routers offer a wireless form of ethernet called WiFi. WiFi works in exactly the same way as ethernet, except that wired NICs need to be replaced with wireless WiFi cards. Having local computers connected wirelessly makes them easy to deploy within a building, although WiFi signals will not carry far and can be blocked by thick walls.

Network security and troubleshooting

Running a network connected to the internet is much more hazardous than just a network of locally connected machines. In theory an intruder from the internet might be able to get into your local machines via your router, just as your local machines use the router to access the internet.

There are two very important steps to take in basic network security. The first is to change the default password on the router to something that only you know. The router's control software will allow you to do this. Default passwords are a well-known way into poorly set-up networks. The second measure to take is to activate the firewall on the router. All good routers should come with a firewall. This facility can monitor and/or block traffic through the router passing to and from the internet and your local network. Firewalls normally come with a default setting, which allows out any local connections but blocks all incoming connections except those requested by local machines.

If you are running a wireless (WiFi) network then you will need to protect your network against unauthorized machines connecting. This is done in two ways: one way is to list the MAC addresses of machines permitted to connect to your router. The second is to enable Wireless Encryption Protocol (WEP) on your router. This will create a 'key' that needs to be stored on all local machines you wish to use that wireless router connection.

Network troubleshooting can be divided into two sets of problems: those on your local (organizational) network and those on the internet. Both types are potentially hard to deal with. For local problems the best that you can do is to clearly diagnose a problem (for example, 'Network printer type X is no longer printing files sent to it') and try and find a fix for that problem via Google searches (see 'Troubleshooting', p.59).

Internet-related problems can either be the fault of your internet service provider (ISP), in which case you can contact them with the problem, or they might be a fault somewhere else on the internet, in which case you can only wait for them to be resolved or try some alternative service. The most useful facility for diagnosing internet problems is a utility called 'traceroute'. What it does is show you each device on the internet that traffic from your machine to another machine (such as a website) traverses. Using this display you can see where the problem occurs, with your ISP, with an intermediate stage or with the final site you are trying to access. The traceroute display will show where a break occurs.

From the command prompt in Windows one can run traceroute by typing tracert and then the name of the destination site (for example www.google.com if you cannot connect to Google). There are also utility suites that include traceroute and public traceroute sites provided by some ISPs.

Activity 21

Try doing a tracert from your machine to www.google.com. Can you work out where the intermediate devices are located from their names?

Download a package called Sam Spade from www.samspade.org, which provides a friendly traceroute feature and a whole host of other diagnostic tools for internet problems. Try this out.

For a global listing of browser-based traceroute tools, which can route to a destination site and also back to your site (if you know its domain name or IP address) see www.traceroute.org/.

The London Internet Exchange, the main switching point for internet traffic into and out of the UK, provides traceroute and other tools at www.linx.net/tools/index.thtml.

Evaluation of services: analysing surveys using Excel

Software for survey analysis can be extremely expensive, which combined with a lack of training in how to analyse surveys is in many cases why only a handful of staff in many organizations are involved in survey work. This really does not need to be the case, as with the expansion of ICT provision in libraries community library staff are well equipped to evaluate their services regularly. In fact Excel offers such a sophisticated package that it allows easy analysis of even complex survey data using a system called Pivot Tables, sometimes referred to as Frequency Tables.

Simply put, pivot tables analyse spreadsheet data by counting the number of occurrences of a particular option, or in other words the frequency of occurrence of an option.

Designing a survey

To highlight the issues in using pivot tables we need to first design a simple survey. This survey will be short and ask questions related to the customers' use of ICT in the library. Obviously when developing your own survey feel free to add more questions where you see fit, and experiment with question types.

Pivot tables work best when you wish to analyse specific categories of data. For instance, if you were asking a question on a survey related to demographic information, the following set-up would be easily analysed in a pivot table:

1. Sex: Male   Female (Circle one)
2. Age: Under 12 12–16   17–25   26–40   41–60   60+ (Circle one)

For a pivot table to work successfully, any responses to the questions above need to be coded. This is actually a very straightforward process; essentially it involves giving each possible response to a question a numerical value when entering the results onto a spreadsheet. For example, question 1 asks if the respondents are male or female. A simple code for this question would be 1 = Male and 2 = Female. It is very important that the coding for a survey is determined before the survey data is entered onto the spreadsheet, otherwise it can be easy to become confused by which numbers were used where for which specific option. It is good practice to create a guide to the codes used once the survey is complete, as this makes data entry of the results very straightforward.

The next few questions will seek responses related to service use. For each potential response, a code has been typed in beside each option. These will be the codes used when entering data onto the spreadsheet:

3. On average how often to you use the library? (Circle one)
Every day 1   Two to three times a week 2   Once a week 3
Once every two weeks 4   Once a month 5   Less than once a month 6

4. On average how often do you use the computer facilities when you visit the library? (Circle one)
Every visit 1   On every second visit 2   On every third visit 3
Once every four visits 4   I rarely use the computing facilities 5
I never use the computing facilities 6

5. Which activity do you undertake most when using the computers? (Circle one)
Internet 1   Word processing 2   Spreadsheets 3   Databases 4
E-mail 5   Scanning pictures 6   Presentations 7   CD-ROMs 8

6. On a scale of 1 to 5, 1 being Very Satisfied and 5 being Very Unsatisfied, how satisfied are you with the computing facilities on offer in the library?

Very Satisfied				Very Unsatisfied
1 —	2 —	3 —	4 —	5

7. Are there any computing facilities not on offer that you would like to see in the library?

_____

_____

_____

Thank you for your time in completing this survey.

Once the survey has been designed it is very important to pilot it with other staff members before you issue it to customers. They will often identify ambiguous questions you may have missed. Open questions, where you elicit more details in

THE IMPORTANCE OF BUILDING ON ICT SKILLS 69

the responses, are unlikely to be able to be analysed using pivot tables, but you can still type such responses onto the spreadsheet in order that you have complete responses in one file.

For the purposes of this exercise, 20 survey responses have been entered onto the spreadsheet to enable us to run some pivot tables and elicit results. When entering data it is important that your spreadsheet has categories for each question in the top row that reflect each question. An example spreadsheet for the survey above is highlighted in Figure 3.2.

Figure 3.3 shows what the spreadsheet looks like when data from 20 completed surveys have been entered.

	A	B	C	D	E	F	G	H
1	Sex	Age	Visits	Using PCs	Activities Undertaken	Satisfaction with Service	Other facilities would like to see	
2								
3								
4								
5								

Figure 3.2 Example survey spreadsheet before completion

	A	B	C	D	E	F	G	H
1	Sex	Age	Visits	Using PCs	Activities Undertaken	Satisfaction with Service	Other facilities would like to see	
2	2	4	2	5	1	2	More computers	
3	2	3	3	6	1	3	Less computers	
4	2	5	4	5	1	2	More staff help	
5	2	5	3	6	1	3		
6	2	6	4	3	1	4		
7	2	6	3	2	1	3		
8	2	3	2	4	5	4		
9	2	2	2	3	5	3		
10	2	2	3	4	5	2		
11	1	6	4	3	1	3		
12	2	4	3	3	1	4	Less noise from children	
13	1	5	4	1	1	3		
14	1	5	5	1	2	1		
15	1	1	5	1	2	1		
16	1	1	4	2	6	3		
17	1	4	3	4	1	2		
18	1	3	4	3	5	3		
19	1	2	3	2	1	2		
20	1	1	3	1	1	1	More games	

Figure 3.3 Example survey spreadsheet with data from 20 completed surveys

With the data entered, we can now begin to analyse the spreadsheet and produce results. To start the process:

1 Select the **Data** option from the top menu, and click on **Pivot Table and Pivot Chart Report**
2 This now presents you with a wizard to enable you to create the pivot table. Click **Next**, as we are happy with the default settings on the first screen, which are telling us that we are creating a pivot table from the current spreadsheet.

This is confirmed on the screen that follows, see Figure 3.4.

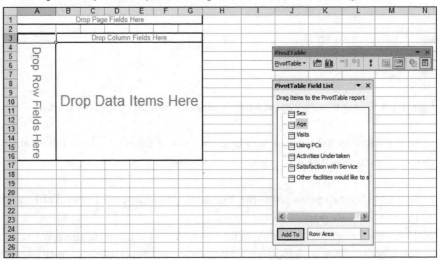

	A	B	C	D	E	F	G	H
1	Sex	Age	Visits	Using PCs	Activities Undertaken	Satisfaction with Service	Other facilities would like to see	
2	2	4	2	5	1		2 More computers	
3	2	3	3	6	1		3 Less computers	
4	2	5	4	5	1		2 More staff help	
5	2	5	3	6	1		3	
6	2	6	4	3	1		4	
7	2	6	3	2	1		3	
8	2	3	2	4	5		4	
9	2	2	2	3	5		3	
10	2	2	3	4	5		2	
11	1	6	4	3	1		3	
12	2	4	3	3	1		4 Less noise from children	
13	1	5	4	1	1		3	
14	1	5	5	1	2		1	
15	1	1	5	1	2		1	
16	1	1	4	2	6		3	
17	1	4	3	4	1		2	
18	1	3	4	3	5		3	
19	1	2	3	2	1		3	
20	1	1	3	1	1			

Figure 3.4 Creating a pivot table from a spreadsheet

3 Click **Next** to continue with the creation of the table. Step 3 in the wizard asks us where we want the pivot table to be created – you can place it into the current sheet, or create a new one. For this exercise we will use the default option, which is creating a new worksheet. The next step is to click the **Finish** button.

This presents you with your blank pivot table, as shown in Figure 3.5.

Figure 3.5 A blank pivot table

The table on the right in Figure 3.5 titled **PivotTable Field List** is the list of categories from the survey data. To create the table, you merely drag and drop the categories into the pivot table. Dragging and dropping the **Sex** field into **Row Fields** and **Data Items** produces the table shown in Figure 3.6.

3	Count of Age	
4	Age ▼	Total
5	1	4
6	2	3
7	3	3
8	4	3
9	5	4
10	6	3
11	Grand Total	20

Figure 3.6 Example of a pivot table showing count of age

One thing to watch out for is in the top left-hand corner of the table. In the example shown in Figure 3.6 it states **Count of Age**, but sometimes the default can be **Sum of Age**, meaning that the column has had all of the options added rather than counted. Ensure that this says Count, and by clicking on the top left-hand corner and selecting Count from the resulting drop-down menu that appears. Obviously this has given us details of the numbers of respondents in each age group, and you should now type in the categories into the table, for example Under 12 to replace 1, 12–16 to replace 2, and the like. It is now straightforward to create a graph from the table using the Chart Wizard button, available from the Pivot Table options box (Figure 3.7).

Figure 3.7 Pivot Table options box

The resulting graph can then be copied and pasted into a Word document for any report you wish to write.

More sophisticated analysis can be done using pivot tables. The pivot table in Figure 3.8 was created by dragging and dropping **Age** and **Visits** into the **Data Items** section, and **Age** into the **Row Fields** and entering the categories into the table.

From this pivot table we are able to compare responses in much more detail, looking for patterns in the data such as frequency of use by specific age groups. Experiment with the creation of tables and graphs illustrating relationships between the data. Tables that compare different fields against each other are sometimes referred to as contingency tables.

3	Count of Visits	Visits				
4	Age	Two to Three times a week	Once a week	Once every two weeks	Once a month	Grand Total
5	Under 12		1	2	1	4
6	12-16	1	2			3
7	17-25	1	1	1		3
8	26-40	1	2			3
9	41-60		1	2	1	4
10	60+		1	2		3
11	Grand Total	3	8	7	2	20

Figure 3.8 Example of a pivot table showing count of visits

Further activities

Create pivot tables and graphs that illustrate the following:

* age group versus satisfaction with service
* sex versus use of PCs
* sex versus frequency of use.

Conclusion – keeping up to date

Nothing dates faster than computer knowledge. Keeping up to date is vital as is trying to expand the range of computer topics one knows about. A good solution is to subscribe to one or more online 'zines' or mailing lists which cover computer developments and problems from a practical point of view. For a list see: http://directory.google.com/Top/Computers/Publications/Magazines_and_E-zines/E-zines/

Another excellent resource for potential computer problems in a library setting is the People's Network mailing list. This is a well-used e-mail list where troubleshooting questions and advice is readily shared among colleagues across the UK who are responsible for managing ICT in libraries.

Activity 22

Visit the homepage of the People's Network mailing list (www.jiscmail.ac.uk/lists/PEOPLESNETWORK.html) and sign up.

Have a browse through the list archives and familiarize yourself with the types of issues discussed.

References

Dodd, C., Baigent, H. and Woodhouse, S. (eds) (2002) *NOF ICT Training Programme for Public Library Staff. Interim survey of training to meet Expected Outcomes*

2–8 and advanced levels of the programme, London, Resource, www.peoplesnet-work.gov.uk/training/id598rep.pdf [accessed 12 September 2003].

ECDL (2003) *European Computer Driving Licence Website*, www.ecdl.co.uk [accessed 9 September 2003].

Garrod, P. (2001) Staff Training and End-user Training Issues within the Hybrid Library, *Library Management*, **22** (1/2), 30–6.

Great Britain. Department for Education and Employment (1997) *Connecting the Learning Society*, London, DfEE.

Great Britain Department for Education and Employment (1998a) *The Learning Age: a renaissance for new Britain*, London, DfEE.

Great Britain Department for Education and Employment (1998b) *Open for Learning, Open for Business*. London, DfEE.

JISCmail (2003) JISCmail Website. National Academic Mailing List Service, www.jiscmail.ac.uk [accessed 5 September 2003].

Library and Information Commission (LIC) (1997) *New Library: the People's Network*, www.ukoln.ac.uk/services/lic/newlibrary [accessed 18 August 2003].

Library and Information Commission (LIC) (1998) *Building the New Library Network: a report to Government*, www.lic.gov.uk/publications/policyreports/building [accessed 1 August 2003].

McNicol, S. (2002) Learning in Libraries: lessons for staff, *New Library World*, **102** (7/8), 251–8.

Ondari-Okemwa, E. (2000) Training Needs of Practising Professional Librarians in the Kenyan Public University Libraries: a critical analysis, *Library Management*, **21** (5), 257–68.

Ormes, S. and Dempsey, L. (1995) *Library and Information Commission Public Library Internet Survey*, www.ukoln.ac.uk/services/papers/ukoln/ormes-1995-01 [accessed 7 September 2003].

Ormes, S. and McClure, C. (1996) *A Comparison of Public Library Internet Connectivity in the USA and UK*, www.ukoln.ac.uk/publib/USAUK1.htm [accessed 7 September 2003].

Poulter, A., Hiom, D. and McMenemy, D. (2005) *The Library and Information Professional's Internet Companion*, London, Facet Publishing.

Spacey, R. E. (2003) An Evaluation of the New Opportunities Fund ICT Training Programme for Public Library Staff, UK, *World Library and Information Congress: 69th IFLA General Conference and Council, Berlin 1–9 August, 2003*, www.ifla.org/IV/ifla69/papers/004e-Spacey.pdf [accessed 19 August 2003].

Spacey, R., Goulding, A. and Murray, I. (2003) ICT and Change in UK Public Libraries: does training matter?, *Library Management*, **24** (1/2), 61–9.

4 Supporting electronic government: a role for public libraries

Alan Poulter and Paul Anderson

Electronic government (e-government) is a current worldwide development aimed at improving interaction between the citizen and his or her government. The principle is that ICTs allow governments to be more contactable and transparent. ICTs also allow government services to be streamlined: publication of documents and completion of government forms can all be done online, aiding speed and efficiency. As will be discussed below, the UK government set a target for all services that could be made available electronically to be accessible in this way by 2005. The opportunity is there and is being grasped by public libraries as they place themselves in the role of intermediary between citizen and access to e-government services. Yet for public libraries to do so, some knowledge of how the e-government sites work and just what types of information they are actually delivering is vital.

This chapter has two main goals:

- to discuss the background to e-government in the UK and allow the reader to delve into some UK e-government sites for familiarization
- to highlight how public libraries can take a central role in providing access to e-government services for their customers through the case study of the Scottish Parliament initiative aimed at using partner libraries in the public libraries sector.

E-government in the UK

As highlighted above, it is government policy to provide UK citizens and businesses with web-based online access to national and local government services by 2005. Local and national government information systems must 'join up', so that their services are seen as a unitary whole by the public. Those services must be made easily accessible, so web-based information and services must be designed for simplicity and ease of use by all. As well as better service delivery via e-services, e-government should improve communication and interaction between government and its electorate ('e-democracy'), and enable government to deal more efficiently with its suppliers ('e-procurement'). E-government should also address social inclusion issues by, for example, making information available in a wider variety of formats than is possible with print.

In 1999, 40% of the 467 UK councils at or above district size did not have a web presence. Central government made council websites the subject of one of its targets for major change when it promised that all services would be available electronically by 2005. Each year the Society of IT Management (Socitm), the professional association for locally based IT managers, examines council websites: its first report produced the figure above. The Better Connected survey for 2003 found for the first time that all councils have a website.

Public libraries are a highly visible, community-based service provided by local authorities, and so have a front-line role to play in the delivery of local e-government in their respective communities. By offering access to the internet and support for acquiring ICT skills, public libraries have a crucial role to play in enabling local people to access and use online e-government services. They already have a mission to promote social inclusion, which e-government can enhance, and are well positioned in the community to address e-democracy issues.

Local e-government

In England and Wales, at local authority level strategies for implementing local e-government are defined in 'Implementing Electronic Government Statements' (IEGs). In Scotland, the equivalent strategies are called '21st Century Government Action Plans'. They summarize the progress an authority has made in implementing e-government, in terms of its success in e-service delivery, e-procurement efforts and e-democracy. Models for these plans have been published by:

Office of the Deputy Prime Minister: e-government @ local homepage
www.localegov.gov.uk/page.cfm?pageID=74&language=eng

Scottish Executive: 21st Century Government
www.scotland.gov.uk/Topics/Government/Open-scotland

There are other yardsticks to judge council progress towards e-government. The Audit Commission (Audit Scotland in Scotland) runs comprehensive performance assessments on the range of council services, including their e-government efforts, while the 'Best Value Performance Indicator 157' (BVPI 157) specifically covers e-government. Despite the plethora of audit processes, quality still varies widely.

Activity 1

Two examples of local council reports on progress towards e-government follow. How useful would they be to a member of the public? How useful do you find them?

Borough of Charnwood: Implementing Electronic Government Statement
www.charnwoodbc.gov.uk/charnwood/ieg/

North Lanarkshire: 21st Century Government Action Plan
www.northlan.gov.uk/your+council/council+departments/chief+executives+office/
docres_north+lanarkshire+direct_21st+century+government+action+plan.html

Try and find your local council's progress report by a web search.

Local council websites

What can local council websites offer? The areas of advantage fall under the headings of access and efficiency

Access

People expect 24 hours-a-day and seven days a week access to services of all kinds, and do not want to queue for an answer, therefore a self-service website is ideal. Just over half of UK adults have internet access, and increasingly will use it in preference to other channels of communication. Technologies like interactive digital television (iDTV) and 3G (third generation) mobile phones promise to spread internet access further. For those without home (or work) access to the internet, access can be through physical outlets, such as kiosks or public libraries.

Efficiency

Several councils place the same information on the website and their internal network (or intranet), and use it as a knowledge base for those answering the phones. Automated processing of transactions online is a particularly good way of saving money, especially if the service is used by sufficient numbers. The cost per visit is very small, compared with other kinds of communication such as printed material or phone calls – although there is little worse than promoting a website and then not having the web server capacity to deal with its popularity.

Local e-government is not only about providing services via the web, it is also about engaging local people in the democratic process – effective local democracy should be the driver for the standard of services delivered by local councils. Internet technologies can help people take part in local planning and political debates in many ways, ranging from public access to council information and minutes of meetings, through online discussion forums to e-voting. As well as voters, e-government should support local councillors, giving them better access to information, policy-making and access to their constituents. E-mail and online discussions can also help to make councillors more accessible to, and better informed about, a broader selection of electors.

Activity 2

NB Part of this exercise was adapted from the methodology used by Socitm's Better Connected survey at: www.socitm.gov.uk/Public/insight/publications/Better+ Connected+03.htm.

Put yourself in the following roles when browsing your local council's website:

- a person leaving school
- a person planning visit to area
- a person caring for an elderly relative
- a person living in social housing.

How easy/hard is it to find information that the above individuals would want? Think about your experience in terms of:

- Access to the council – what information on services is given? Is it clear and easy to follow?
- Joined-up government – are services presented from the customer, not provider, point of view?
- Usability – could the desired information be found by following a short trail of obvious links?

- Currency of information – is the information correct and up-to-date as far as you are aware? Are there statements on pages showing 'last updated on' etc?
- Interactive applications – are contact names and details (address, phone numbers and e-mail addresses) given? Are there online forms available for requesting services?

You might look to like at the following three trailblazing councils, whose websites are models for others to follow:

Tameside
www.tameside.gov.uk/

West Lothian
www.wlonline.org/

Wrexham
www.wrexham.gov.uk/

What facilities/services can you find that set these apart from your local council's site? What e-democracy activities are there? Which of these activities are going on in public libraries?

National e-government

The UK has a slightly more complex e-government structure due to devolution. There are two portals for the executive branches of government, one for England and Wales at:

www.ukonline.gov.uk

and one for Scotland at:

www.scotland.gov.uk/

The Office of the E-Envoy is leading the drive towards e-government in England and Wales:

www.e-envoy.gov.uk/

while the equivalent site for Scotland is:

www.openscotland.gov.uk/

The respective parliaments have websites:

www.parliament.uk/
www.scottish.parliament.uk/

Central government websites have come under criticism, not least from within e-government circles. According to the latest (2003) *UK Online Annual Report* (Office of the E-Envoy, 2004):

- fewer than one in 12 internet users have ever carried out a transaction with the government online
- three-quarters of the UK online population have never visited a government website at all.

The main reason for this failure according to the report was the lack of a single 'clearly branded and heavily promoted' portal to the 3000 .gov.uk websites. The current UK Online portal 'falls a long way short of providing a single delivery point'. Although 96% of Britain's population were aware of a place where they can readily access the internet, a digital inclusion panel would need to be set up with the aim of ensuring everyone could get online from home in five years time – 'Every home in the UK should have a connection to online services through a digital network by 2008 – whether through a personal computer, DTV, mobile phone or other device.'

Encouraging participation in parliamentary business is proving as problematic as providing services. Opening up democracy over the internet ironically reaches the few rather than the many. Amongst the less well-off social groups fewer than one in five has internet access. Half of all Britons online come from the affluent social groups. However, participation rates in elections are falling and surveys of voters reveal a perception that parliaments are out of touch. The trailblazing public online participation in the formative stages of the Communication Bill (Glover, 2002) has been seen as the standard for the future. One site, www.edemocracy.gov.uk/, is a portal for the latest information on participative e-government. At the time of writing, two MPs are running blogs, personal message boards, in an effort to give them more contact with their constituents:

Richard Allan (MP Sheffield Hallam, Lib-Dem)
www.bigblogger.org.uk/

Tom Watson (MP West Bromwich, Labour)
www.tom-watson.co.uk/

Activity 3

Browse the MP's blogs. Do they give you an insight into how a politician functions?

Try to find sites (if any) for your local councillor/MP/MSP/MEP. How do they encourage participation?

Look at the official parliamentary sites for England/Wales and Scotland. What opportunities do they give for online participation?

E-government standards

Making e-government work requires technology standards. If national and local governments all went their own way then their services would not inter-operate, at least not much beyond all being accessible via a web browser. Extensible Markup Language (XML) is the basis of many of these standards; it will be explained in more detail in Chapter 5. The vital standards are:

* e-Government Interoperability Framework (e-GIF), which contains high level policy statements in the first part and technical policies and XML schemas for the exchange of information between government and individuals or organizations in the second
* e-Government Metadata Standard (e-GMS), which specifies the elements and schemes to be used when creating metadata for government information resources or when implementing search systems for these resources; the e-GMS is based on the Dublin Core standard, which has it origins in the information and library community
* e-Government Gateway, which forms a secure hub for transactions with the public
* Government Category List (GCL), which is a classified list of headings for use with the subject element of the e-GMS. It has been used to create the topic index on the Quick Find page of UK Online: www.ukonline.gov.uk/QuickFind/QuickFind/fs/en.

Activity 4

Try and find the following topics by browsing the topic index at
www.ukonline.gov.uk/QuickFind/QuickFind/fs/en:

- giving up smoking
- the Police Complaints Authority
- the New Opportunities Fund
- keeping your child safe on the internet
- asylum in the UK.

Did you have problems finding any of these? How feasible is it to have a simple but comprehensive subject listing of government services?

Projects like Accessible and Personalised Local Authority Web Sites (APLAWS, www.aplaws.org.uk/plus/pages/home/), Seamless (www.seamless.co.uk) and Life Events Access Project, (LEAP, www.leap.gov.uk) are also working on simple access schemes to local government information.

How do these standards work in practice? Imagine an online application which accepts planning applications. A user would see a web form into which they would enter details of their planning application. Attached files in certain permitted formats (for example for image files) might be needed for things like floor plans. Data and files entered would then be stored in a structured record conforming to an XML schema for this application. Metadata would be added to this record containing the name and e-mail address of the person submitting the application, the address at which planning permission was sought, the nature of the application, the date the application was lodged and details of the type of planning application (residential, business and so on). Types of planning applications would come from a controlled list. This record would be searchable (via applicable metadata fields) so that this application could be retrieved and seen by any interested parties. Its progress through planning permission stages would be tracked and monitored by workflow software, so that it does not get lost or unduly delayed. The applicant could be given a facility to track progress or e-mailed progress updates. Finally its status would be set to either passed or rejected with an explanation. An appeal facility could be offered which would re-use the existing record and re-submit it into an appropriate decision-making process.

By keeping the record in machine-readable form, the inefficiencies and costs of paper-based documentation systems are avoided. By being an XML document, the record can easily be formatted for display on the web (or other systems) and its content can be re-used by other applications (such as a customer-relationship management system investigating user satisfaction with government services). The metadata is there is identify the record and allow it to be found by web search tools, in databases, and so on. Finally the user is empowered by getting an easy way to make an application and keep tabs on its progress.

Although government has set itself this common structure to follow, a recent study found little conformance of central government sites to its own standards (Loney, 2003). Of 62 government sites tested, all but five failed to comply with government standards on metadata (e-GMS) and content (e-GIF). Only five sites had any of the mandatory data, and the best score was just under 5.88% compliant – every other site, including that of the e-Envoy, failed on every single page.

Furthermore, only four of the sites tested passed tests for compliance with the W3C's Web Accessibility Initiative guidelines (see Chapter 5). The Office of the e-Envoy was one of these four government websites. Every one of the other 58 sites failed to meet the basic Priority 1 requirements – the most basic level of accessibility without which, says the W3C, 'one or more groups will find it impossible to access information in the document. Satisfying this checkpoint is a basic requirement for some groups to be able to use Web documents.' Some sites were less than 1% compliant (UK Online itself, the Equal Opportunities Commission, the Home Office site, the Welsh Office and the website for the Prime Minister, whose site scored zero on all compliance tests!).

CASE STUDY

E-government in Scottish public libraries: the Scottish Parliament experience

Author: Paul Anderson, Community Outreach Officer, the Scottish Parliament
From 1999 Paul was Library Liaison Officer at the Scottish Parliament Information Services, where his role was to promote the use of Scottish Parliament publications within the public library network.

Background

Much has been written over the last decade or so about the potential of new information and ICTs to revolutionize democracy and citizen participation in the democratic process. But what is the evidence on the ground that local authority library services, generously supported through the New Opportunities Fund (NOF), have helped to facilitate a citizenship better equipped to become more directly involved with the political decision-making process?

More importantly, what evidence is there that the several millions of pounds of NOF funding channelled through the People's Network into hardware, software and upgraded communication links – not to mention the huge ongoing investment in local authority staff training and development – has resulted in a Scottish citizenship that feels more 'engaged' with the new Parliament and the Executive?

What do we mean by e-governance?

In attempting to gauge whether e-governance initiatives have had an impact in enabling citizens to engage with Scotland's Parliament since May 1999, it might be helpful to consider what is meant by the term 'e-government'. Are we referring to the relatively simplistic 'open banquet' approach, whereby governance agencies (the Scottish Parliament, the Scottish Executive, local authorities and so on) post a wealth of information in the form of countless web pages and then expect citizens to access this information? Or do we mean a more two-way and inclusive approach – where citizens make use of ICTs in public libraries to actively engage in, and contribute to, the democratic process?

A useful starting point may be to identify an acceptable definition of 'e-government', as the terminology is inexact and lends itself, if not to misinterpretation, then certainly to multiple interpretation. Traynor and McLaren (2003) offer a functional interpretation in their three-form definition of e-government:

> access to information – *'the most common form of e-government . . . the exposure of government information on websites'*
> transaction services – *'which provide the opportunities to complete transactions [with] government departments through web-based services'*
> citizen participation – *'the most controversial'* form of e-government . . . *'direct citizen participation in government decision making'*.

This breakdown is useful in that it highlights clearly the different forms of, not only e-governance, but also of 'engagement' with the political process.

Silcock (2001) also provides a helpful summation: 'E-government is the use of technology to enhance the access to and delivery of government services to benefit citizens, business partners and employees . . . it is about building a partnership between governments and citizens . . . At the centre of it all is the customer.'

Few would argue with this last point – or at least, with the aspiration implicit within it.

The public library sector as a crucial enabler

Public libraries are very often at the heart of local communities. In an age of seeming widespread disenchantment with the democratic process at local, national and international level, they are very often the only visible source of governance information in high streets and housing schemes across the country. Particularly in rural areas such as the Scottish Highlands and Islands, for example, public libraries are crucial links to the wider world.

However, with only 50% (www.citizensonline.org.uk/statisticslate.shtml) of households in Scotland enjoying internet access, this begs the question: what about the 50% of households in Scotland that aren't wired up? Might public libraries play a role in filling this gap in providing opportunities for two-way participative e-governance?

Does an 'enhanced access to and delivery of government services' (Silcock) lead to an enhanced quality of life for Scotland's citizens? Do Scotland's citizens feel more involved with the decision-making processes that affect them as a result of hugely increased levels of ICT provision in Scotland's public libraries?

Public disengagement with the political process is a cause of growing concern – witness the 49% (Herbert, Burnside and Curtis, 2003) turnout at the 2003 Scottish Parliament election. However, can enhanced levels of ICTs in public libraries and various parallel e-government initiatives turn the tide? Perhaps an examination of the experiences of the Scottish Parliament's Partner Library Network can provide some insight.

The Partner Library Network

The Partner Library Network is a scheme of 80 public libraries, which act as focal points in local communities for parliamentary information. With one Partner Library in every parliamentary constituency, plus an additional seven (mostly in remote rural areas in the Highlands and Islands) Partner Libraries are one of the most high profile ways in which the Parliament delivers on its commitment to be open, accountable, accessible and participative at a community level.

Partner Libraries receive a wide range of parliamentary information resources and services. These include: official parliamentary publications; access to parliamentary research briefings; a range of educational materials for children, young people and teachers; and a wide array of general information sources in various formats including CD-ROM and video, as well as in Gaelic and other minority languages.

Staff in Partner Libraries receive *in situ* training and support in the use of

Scottish Parliament information resources. They can also make use of the enquiry support service, through the Parliament's library liaison officer, to assist in answering user enquiries.

Every Partner Library provides free public internet access. And like all public libraries, every Partner Library finds that the demand placed on this service often exceeds their ability to supply. But just how much of this new ICT infrastructure is used by citizens to engage in the two-way process of participative e-government?

A key element of the library liaison officer post is to maintain a visibility and accessibility within the public library sector. This involves the library liaison officer visiting each Partner Library regularly (usually every 9–12 months) to meet staff and to discuss uptake of parliamentary information. These are, in effect, inspection visits. In addition, vital management information is acquired through detailed annual surveys where each Partner Library reports on its experiences in delivering on their parliamentary information remit.

The Partner Library experience of e-governance

While national initiatives such as, for example, UKOnline, NHSDirect, Openscotland, ECare and visitscotland suggest there is a wealth of e-government provision available through the Scottish public library sector, experience on the ground reveals a widespread disinclination towards participative e-government on the part of users. Almost without exception, anecdotal evidence supported by findings from annual Partner Library surveys indicates little, if any, visible user-driven e-governance activity – either within the Partner Library context or within the public library sector generally.

What is clear is that demand by end-users in the Partner Library Network (and there is no evidence to suggest the situation is different in non Partner Libraries) for parliamentary information is relatively low-level, simplistic and focuses on contact details for Members of the Scottish Parliament (MSPs) and on information about the Parliament as a visitor attraction.

Partner Libraries – like all public libraries – do not make publicly available records of websites visited by users. However, it is reasonable to expect that an indeterminate number of users will occasionally access governance websites such as those of the local authority, the Scottish Parliament, Scottish Executive or any number of national governance agencies. Certainly the only evidence of e-government engagement visible from visits to Partner Libraries in 80 communities across Scotland is the sporadic (and non-quantified) accessing by library users of governance agency websites.

One of the most widespread user behaviours visible in Partner Libraries is the high proportion of internet use focused on non-learning (and particularly on non-e-government) activity. The evidence in libraries is that the majority of users of these facilities are far more interested in leisure-orientated use than in engaging with the democratic process: leisure 'surfing', downloading of music, e-mailing, instant messaging, online games playing – all are far more in evidence in public libraries than activities focused around participative e-governance.

In addition, very many users use People's Network PCs not for online (internet) use, but for word-processing and the like. Increasingly, school pupils and students in further and higher education are making use of ICT facilities in public libraries in order to escape the strains of demand on the same facilities in traditional educational institutions.

Other more formal analyses confirm the lack of uptake of two-way e-governance through the Partner Library Network: the Dundee SPICe Project examined the degree of uptake of Scottish Parliament information in that city over a six-month period in 2001. Despite surveying numerous libraries and other information providers, as well as a wide range of community groups and voluntary sector organizations, the report's findings revealed little in the way of two-way e-governance activity.

Bucking the trend?

Occasionally Partner Libraries experience peaks in interest as a result of single-issue politics – for example, banning fox hunting, free personal health care for the elderly and land reform. When such issues are in the media spotlight, the Parliament's website also records increased visits. It is clear that wider societal factors (not least the mass media) influence, or even drive, the information demands of end-users.

Likewise, when events have a very real impact on the day-to-day lives of local communities, Partner Libraries report significant increases in interest from users for information regarding what action the Parliament is taking on specific issues. Notable examples include the foot-and-mouth crisis in 2001, which affected large parts of Dumfries and Galloway; and the transfer of Glasgow City Council housing stock in 2002. In both cases, the Partner Libraries in the areas concerned reported increased usage of ICT facilities both to e-mail MSPs directly, and to examine the Parliament's record of debate in each issue. In addition, the Parliament's Public Information Service reported increased numbers of e-mails from members of the public requesting information.

The current lack of uptake of e-government initiatives through the Partner Library Network cannot be wholly attributed to the Parliament or the public library sector. What we have to acknowledge is that this is symptomatic of wider societal factors, best summarized, perhaps, as a widespread apathy and disenchantment with politics, politicians and the political process.

Enhancing opportunities for e-governance

What is clear is that, for the most part, users in Partner Libraries aren't yet engaged in any meaningful way with e-governance and, to date, show little inclination in this direction.

Despite the huge growth in public library ICTs over the past four to six years, most library services would be hard pushed to cite examples of sustained user-driven e-governance activity. Where there are opportunities, however, there is some evidence that take-up is increasing.

The Parliament is proactive in pursuing a number of e-governance initiatives and facilities. The Participation Services Team, for example, is involved in a range of outreach and education programmes aimed at stimulating uptake in civic engagement opportunities. These events are aimed, in particular, at community groups, the voluntary sector, elderly forums, youth groups, ethnic minorities and Gaelic speakers. Partner Libraries are very often the venues for these community outreach events, which aim to promote awareness of the engagement mechanisms available, not least through promoting participation in two-way e-governance opportunities.

The Scottish Parliament is well advanced, relative to other legislatures, in facilitating citizen e-access to the decision-making process. For example, e-mail messages can be sent to every MSP at the simple address: joe.bloggs.msp@scottish. parliament.uk.

In addition, as well as every MSP having their own detailed biographical and constituency contact pages on its website, the Parliament's Have Your Say online forum (www.communitypeople.net/interactive/) demonstrates an active commitment to providing opportunities for e-engagement. This allows members of the public to contribute to a discussion-board-style forum enabling them to express their views directly to Members on matters of parliamentary business currently under consideration.

E-petitioning

Another high-profile example of the Parliament's efforts in this area is in its e-petitioning facility, an area where the Scottish Parliament is recognized as a world leader (OECD, 2004). In February 2004, the Public Petitions Committee formally launched the e-petitioner system, which, uniquely, allows an online debate between MSPs and members of the public with an interest in a petition. The system, which has been developed by the Parliament's statutory Public Petitions Committee in conjunction with Napier University's International Teledemocracy Centre and BT Scotland, allows the petitioner the opportunity to gather support from a much wider constituency than traditional methods.

An e-petition is published on the web for a set period of time before being formally lodged with the Parliament. The Committee will then consider the petition along with a report from the ITC on the extent of support gathered on the web and a summary of the online debate.

The Queensland Parliament in Australia is currently the only other Parliament to allow e-petitions that collect names and addresses over the internet, but the Queensland system does not allow an open discussion of the issue and the petition has to be submitted by an MP. The Scottish Parliament system allows anyone any age to submit an e-petition. The Parliament's commitment to equal opportunities is further demonstrated by the fact that guidance on the use of the e-petitioner system is published in seven different languages.

Figures from the Committee show that, after a slow start, the e-petitioning facility is generating increased interest and activity across a wide range of areas. The first e-petition to the Parliament ('Our Seas Deserve a Vote') started to collect signatures in December 1999. During the first parliamentary session (1999–2003), eight e-petitions were submitted, with a total of 4746 signatories. In the current parliamentary session to date (the period May 2003–January 2004), seven e-petitions have been lodged with 3436 signatories.

The now widespread availability of free public internet access in public libraries offers an ideal opportunity for the Public Petitions Committee and the Participation Services Team to work together through various outreach and education events within the Partner Library context to raise awareness of the e-petitioner facility. An increased number of petitions submitted through the public library sector would be a robust indicator of the potential of the Partner Library Network as an environment through which to promote and engage in e-governance.

In addition, the Parliament is keen to stress its openness to co-operative approaches from other civic agencies aimed at progressing and enhancing opportunities for e-participation.

Conclusion

The case study above highlights how public libraries can play a role in providing a link between government representatives and the citizens. The crucial aspect the library staff play is in knowledge of how to use the resource. While it is not necessary to know which government form is hosted on which website, the ability to understand which portal to use for which stream of government is something that can only be achieved via usage of the sites.

References

Glover, J. (2002) Parliament makes E-history, *Guardian Online*, 23 May, www.guardian.co.uk/internetnews/story/0,7369,720264,00.html.

Herbert, S., Burnside, R. and Curtis, S. (2003) *Election 2003*, Scottish Parliament Information Centre (SPICe) Research Briefing, 03/25, 6 May 2003.

Loney, M. (2003) *Government Sites Continue to Flout Standards*, ZDNet UK, 25 November, http://news.zdnet.co.uk/business/0,39020645,39118102,00.htm.

OECD (2004) *Promise and Problems of E-Democracy: challenges of online citizen engagement*, Organisation for Economic Co-operation and Development, 2004.

Office of the E-Envoy (2004) *UK Online Annual Report – 2003*, London, Office of the E-Envoy, www.cnnic.net.cn/download/manual/international-report/ir_03_uk.pdf [accessed 20 March 2005].

Silcock, R. (2001) What is E-government?, *Parliamentary Affairs*, **54** (1), (January), 88-101.

Traynor, M. and McLaren, R. (2003) *E-government in Scotland: ticking the box or delivering meaningful services to the citizen?*, Conference paper. Fédération Internationale de Géomètres (FIG), Paris, April 13–17.

Notes on case study

The Scottish Parliament is *not* the Scottish government; that responsibility rests in large part with the Scottish Executive. Consequently, the Scottish Parliament does not generate and disseminate *government* information. Instead it deals with *parliamentary* information. This may seem an overly pedantic point, but it is an important one in a society where most citizens are not aware of the crucial distinction between government and parliament. Suffice to say that both the Scottish Parliament and the Scottish Executive generate and disseminate *governance* information. This article refers to *e-governance* in the widest sense.

Each month, the Scottish Parliament website typically receives in the region of 750,000 hits from 50,000 unique visitors. Source: Scottish Parliament Web Master.

The Dundee SPICe Project was funded by the Scottish Library and Information Council, in order to identify best practice in promoting and raising awareness of access to parliamentary information in Dundee. The unpublished report is available at www.dundeecity.gov.uk/centlib/spicereport.pdf.

Section 3

Content creation in the 21st-century public library

5 Designing websites and intranets and understanding XML

Alan Poulter and David McMenemy

Introduction

One of the main advantages that library and information staff have always had is that we understand information, both its role and how people seek it. As trite as this may seem, in the information age there is nothing quite as important as that as a starting point. When we consider the world wide web and view some of the overly technical or graphically hungry pages therein it is sometimes easy to forget that all the web is there to do is to impart information. Breaking it down to that simple fact, it becomes clear that an understanding of how to create web pages is an essential skill for any library and information worker who wishes to package information in the digital age.

This chapter attempts to give grounding in world wide web (hereafter referred to as web) and related technologies. It starts by discussing why public library staff would want to be involved in creating web resources, moves on to looking at HTML, then website design, then shifts onto site management and finally looks at Extensible Markup Language (XML).

For those readers interested in a more detailed coverage of internet-related topics please see *The Library and Information Professional's Internet Companion* (Poulter, Hiom and McMenemy, 2005).

Creating pages for the web and intranets

It is no accident that many local authorities have consulted public library staff about the creation of corporate websites, with some even placing library staff in charge of creation and management of the entire site. Forward-thinking authorities realized early on in the push for e-government that library staff had the skills necessary to develop excellent information resources. The technical aspects to building a website can be overrated; really all that is needed is some time spent learning HTML, and even this can be bypassed if an efficient web editing package is purchased, such as Front Page or Dreamweaver. It certainly is tempting to buy a web editor, but some time learning basic HTML before the purchase makes you a much more efficient user of the software, as you can troubleshoot problems very quickly. Web editors such as Dreamweaver and Front Page are known as WYSI-WYG editors, short for 'what you see is what you get.' Essentially these programs allow you to create a web page while viewing it exactly the way anyone would see it while using a web browser. Both editors work much more smoothly, however, when the user is aware of what HTML tags work for each circumstance.

Another point to bear in mind is that although the instructions below discuss HTML and involve you in creating pages in the context of the web, the technologies are just as useful and transferable across a local area network (LAN) intranet system. Therefore learning web design does not entail you working on a website; you could merely be creating pages of links and information for your local library, staff or customer. There are many reasons why you may wish to do this. First, consider creation of frequently asked question pages (FAQs) for information on the local area or the library, or for specific queries that you are commonly asked. You may also wish to promote the creation of local newsletters for community groups using HTML pages. If you cannot find web space for these pages, storing on a local library server for viewing them in the library is an equally good way for local residents to read the information while visiting the library. Another reason you may wish to learn how to create web pages is to teach the skills yourself in classes run within the library.

HTML

Hypertext Markup Language is a platform independent language that enables web browsers to display files in a standard format on a monitor. The basic component of the language is a tag, which informs the browser how to display data, for instance describing the size, style and positioning in the document. In publishing terms these specifications are called the 'markup'. The most current specification is HTML Version 4.0. For this specification please see www.w3.org/TR/REC-html40/.

Apart from a few exceptions, tags come in pairs, an opening and closing tag, which encapsulate the text to be displayed in a particular style. The opening and closing tag are almost identical apart from the forward slash (/) in the closing tag. For example, the following HTML statement:

<B>The Internet</B> is the fastest growing computer network in the world.

will be displayed as:

The Internet is the fastest growing computer network in the world.

Every HTML document must contain some standard tags to define its major components. The <HTML> and </HTML> indicate the beginning and end of an HTML document. An HTML document consists of a heading section and a body section. The heading section mostly contains the title of the document that will be displayed in the title section by the browser. The heading section is identified by the tags <HEAD> and </HEAD>, and the title tags are <TITLE> and </TITLE>. The body section contains the main text and images of the document, and is identified by <BODY> and </BODY>. Therefore a basic HTML document will look something like this:

```
<HTML>
<HEAD>
<TITLE>My home page</TITLE>
</HEAD>
<BODY>
This web page will contain information about me.
    </BODY>
    </HTML>
```

Activity 1

An HTML document can be created using any text editor or word processor on any platform. For these activities you should use Notepad, available in Windows XP.

IMPORTANT: Make sure that when you save your file, you give it an .html extension (for instance index.html) to enable the web browser to recognize it as an HTML document.

It is considered good practice to write all tags in capital letters, as this will help you to help identify tags and follow the HTML structure.

You will find Notepad via Start button and Accessories.

Create your own home page by the typing the basic HTML document above into Notepad. Save your file as index.html. Open a web browser and select Open the File menu, then click on Browse to find your file called index.html. The browser will interpret the HTML tags and display index.html as a web page.

In Notepad edit index.html, putting your name as the title and adding basic information about yourself (name, date of birth, address and phone number) in the body. To view your changes after saving index.html you must click the Reload/Refresh button in the browser.

Formatting an HTML document

You will have noticed that adding text to the body of a web page simply causes that text to be displayed as a solid body. There are a large number of tags that allow you to format the text in your document. A few of these formatting tags are described below.

Headings are used to indicate new sections and subsections with tags like <H1> and </H1>. HTML offers six heading levels numbered <H1> to <H6>, where <H1> is used for the main heading, and <H6> for the lowest level of heading.

Paragraphs can be defined using just <P>, and indicate a block of text. This is relevant as a browser ignores any hard returns (carriage returns or line breaks), indentations or blank lines in HTML documents. This feature also enables you to lay out your source text in such a way that is easy to read for you, for example starting each tag on a new line.

The centre tags <CENTER> and </CENTER> can be used to centre items, e.g.

```
<CENTER>This is a centred paragraph.<P></CENTER>
```

which would be displayed as follows:-

This is a centred paragraph.

IMPORTANT: note the US spelling of the CENTER tag!

Text can be formatted as bold by using the <B> and </B> tags, as italics by using the <I> and </I> tags, and underlined by using the <U> and </U> tags. Note that underlines are used by default to indicate links.

This type of style tags is called a physical style tag. There is another type of style called logical style. Logical style tags format text according to the meaning of its attributes on the browser style sheet. For instance the logical style element <em> for emphasis would generally be displayed as italics, unless defined differently on the style sheet. Common logical style tags are <EM> and </EM> for emphasis (usually displayed as italics), <STRONG> and </STRONG> for strong emphasis (usually displayed as bold), <CITE> and </CITE> for citation (usually displayed as italics).

If you want to include a line break with no extra space between lines (such as the <P> tag would define) you can use the <BR> tag. This is one of the few tags that does not require a closing tag, for example:

```
Line one<BR>Line two
```

would appear as:

> Line one
> Line two

A horizontal black line can be added for example after a section of text with the single <HR> tag (horizontal rule).

You can add comments to your HTML document that can help you or somebody else to understand and modify the structure of the document. A browser will not display comments. Comments are encapsulated by one tag as follows:

```
<!—This is a comment—>
```

You can change the background colour by adding an attribute to the <BODY> tag. For example, <BODY BGCOLOR="BLUE"> will change the background to blue.

The colour of text can be changed by modifying the <BODY> tag to read for instance <BODY TEXT="RED">.

These tags can be combined in to one tag, for instance <BODY BGCOLOR ="RED" TEXT="BLACK">.

Colours are represented either by their names or as a six-digit hexadecimal value, showing RGB values. You can find sample colours and their values at www.hidaho.com/colorcenter.

IMPORTANT: note the US spelling of the BGCOLOR tag!

To create an unnumbered list, which uses bullet points, use the paired tags <UL> and </UL> which encapsulate a number of list items, identified by the single tag <LI>. For example:

```
<UL>
<LI> first item
<LI> second item
<LI> third item
</UL>
```

which will be displayed as:

> • first item
> • second item
> • third item

Numbered lists (or ordered lists) are created in exactly the same way as unnumbered lists but required the tag pairs <OL> and </OL>, which encapsulate a number of list items <LI>.

Lists can be nested (i.e. contain other lists) by using embedded list tags. For example:

```
<UL>
<LI> first item
<UL>
<LI> first subitem
<LI> second subitem
</UL>
<LI> second item
<LI> third item
</UL>
```

which will be displayed as:

> • first item
>   — first subitem
>   — second subitem
> • second item
> • third item

Activity 2

Expand and enhance index.html to incorporate each of the features discussed above. After each change, save index.html, and then reload and view it from the browser to see the effect of your change.

Images

The most common type of image files are gif and jpg files. As you will know from viewing experience, incorporating images on pages will slow down the time it takes to display that page. You should therefore be careful in selecting images to include in your documents. This does not tend to be such a problem if the pages are loading from an intranet system.

The tag used to include an image is:

```
<IMG SRC="image.gif">
```

The above example assumes that your graphics file image.gif is in exactly the same directory as your web page. If it is not then you need to precede the graphics file name with a directory path.

You can specify how text and image should be aligned. By default following text will align with the bottom of the image. You can also specify top and middle alignment using the following format:

```
<IMG SRC="image.gif" ALIGN=TOP> Text to be displayed
```
or
```
<IMG SRC="image.gif" ALIGN=MIDDLE> Text to be dis-
played
```

Images without text can be aligned by making them a separate paragraph.

You can also change the background to a graphic (GIF or JPG) file. The `<BODY>` tag will become `<BODY BACKGROUND="image.gif">`. Note that this overrides a BGCOLOR setting.

IMPORTANT: Images from web pages can be saved to disk by right clicking on an image in your browser and then choosing Save to disk. Save images in the same directory in which you are storing your web pages.

Activity 3

Have a look at:

www.iconbazaar.com/
www.webplaces.com/search/
www.ditto.com/

and download some interesting/appropriate icons/images/etc from these sites and incorporate them into your web page.

Linking HTML documents

The hypertext element of HTML enables you to create links to different areas within the same document, or to other documents. These hyperlinks can be text or an image and can usually be identified because they are a different colour, underlined, or the cursor changes to the pointed finger. The hypertext link tags are <A> and </A> for anchor.

A hyperlink to another document needs to contain the URL (uniform resource locator) for the document. This can be an absolute address – the full URL, for example www.strath.ac.uk/filename.html, or a relative filename to a file in for instance your own directory, just filename.html.

The hyperlink format is:

```
<A HREF="filename.html">This text will be underlined
as a link</A>
```

where <A> is the opening tag for a hyperlink, and within that tag HREF followed by the URL defines the file address. In this example the text 'This text will be underlined as a link' is the highlighted hyperlink in the document, and </A> is the end tag.

The hyperlink format for absolute URLs is:

```
<A HREF="www.strath.ac.uk/filename.html">This text
will be underlined as a link</A>
```

You can use graphics as links to other pages by embedding the image tag in a link. For instance:

```
<A HREF="filename.html"><IMG SRC="image.gif"></A>
```

IMPORTANT: you should always use no more than eight letters, all lowercase, for your file names. Always use the extension .html to indicate HTML files and .gif/.jpg for graphics files. The reason for this is to ensure compatibility across different computers and operating systems.

Hyperlinks can also be used to link to a specific section of a document. To do this, these specific sections need to have named anchors to which the links can refer. These named anchors are created by including the tags <A NAME> and </A>. For instance, to create a link within a document, first place the named anchor:

```
<A NAME="sechead1">Section Heading One</A>
```

where Section Heading has now been named identifier. This will enable the creation of a link to the section as follows:

```
<A HREF="#sechead1">Underlined link to Section
Heading One</A>
```

where the hyperlink 'Underlined link to Section Heading One' will link to Section Heading One.

The two techniques of linking can be combined by creating the following hyperlink:

```
<A HREF="otherdoc.html#sechead1"> Underlined link to
Section Heading One in otherdoc.html</A>
```

You can also include hyperlinks enabling the user to send mail to you or any other email address with the mailto attribute in a hyperlink. For example:

```
<A HREF="mailto:david.mcmenemy@anywhere.co.uk">Send
Email to David McMenemy</A>
```

will send e-mail to david.mcmenemy@anywhere.co.uk when clicking on 'Send Email to David McMenemy'.

Activity 4

Create a link to an external URL, for instance your library home page.

Save index.html with a new page title to distinguish it (e.g. New page) and a new file name, newpage.html, so that you now have two web pages. Create links between these two pages. Add anchors to both pages and create links to these.

Create a mail back hyperlink to your own email address and create a hyperlink from an image.

See if you can work out the html to add an image to your page using a hyperlink.

Tables

Tables display information in a tabular form. Tables are defined in HTML by the `<TABLE>` and `</TABLE>` tags.

A table can be given a border as an attribute of the `<TABLE>` tag, for instance `<TABLE BORDER="1">`, where 1 indicates the line thickness.

Within tables you can specify title or caption for a table with the `<CAPTION>` and `</CAPTION>` tags.

Rows are defined by `<TR>` and `</TR>` tags at the beginning and end of each row. Within table rows you can define individual cells with the `<TD>` and `</TD>` tags. Columns can be given header cells with the tags `<TH>` and `</TH>`, which will automatically be displayed as bold and centred.

An example table may be defined as follows:

```
<TABLE BORDER="1">
<CAPTION>Table title</CAPTION>
<TR>
    <TH>first header</TH>
    <TH>second header</TH>
</TR>
<TR>
    <TD>item 1</TD>
    <TD>item 2</TD>
</TR>
<TR>
    <TD>item A</TD>
    <TD>item B</TD>
</TR>
</TABLE>
```

Activity 5

In index.html display your job history as a list; in newpage.html display this information in a table.

Frames

Frames are individual, independently scrolling regions of a web page. The content that each frame displays is determined by a distinct URL, and frames can be targeted by other URLs within the same window. Useful applications of frames are for instance a static frame, which displays a page that is always visible while the content in the other frame(s) changes; or a frame with a table of content, which links to pages that will be displayed in an adjacent frame.

An HTML document is created whose sole purpose is to define the layout of the frames that make up the page using the <FRAMESET> and </FRAMESET> tags. This HTML document is often very simple and does not contain the <BODY tag>. In this document you define how you want the frames to be divided on the screen, and you specify which HTML document you want displayed in each of the frames.

To divide the screen in two columns use the COLS tag followed by the percentages of the screen you want each column to occupy, for instance:

```
<FRAMESET COLS="30%,70%">
```

will create two columns, the left one occupying 30% of the screen, and the right one the remainder. Similarly screens can be split horizontally using the ROWS tag. Frames can be further split using nested frames. The <FRAMESET> tag can be further modified with the BORDER and FRAMEBORDER tag to include visible lines around frames, for example:

```
<FRAMESET BORDER=1 FRAMEBORDER=1 COLS="30%, 70%>
```

To display HTML documents in a frame the single <FRAME> tag is used for each of the frames. The format is:

```
<FRAME SRC="fileone.html" NAME="contentpage"
SCROLLING="NO">
<FRAME SRC="filetwo.html" NAME="mainwindow" SCROLL-
BARS="AUTO">
```

The first column will display the HTML document fileone.htm that contains a page of contents, and has been named contentpage. No scrollbar will be displayed in this window. The second column will display HTML document filetwo.htm that contains the main text, and which has been named mainwindow. Scrollbars will be used if necessary. A frameset is an HTML page that simply lists how many frames are shown and initially what pages are shown within each frame.

A typical HTML document for a frame set, called frameset.html, will be like this:

```
<HTML>
<HEAD>
<title>Frame set</title>
</HEAD>
<FRAMESET COLS="20%,80%">
<FRAME SRC="left.html" NAME="left_window"
SCROLLING="no">
<FRAME SRC="index.html" NAME="right_window">
</FRAMESET>
</HTML>
```

Note how each window in the frame is named, so that links can be made to change the page displayed in these windows if wanted. The file left.html will be:

```
<HTML>
<HEAD>
<title>Left Window</title>
</HEAD>
<body>
<A HREF="index.html" TARGET="right_window">Personal
Information with job list</A><P>
<A HREF="newpage.html" TARGET="right_window">Personal
Information with job table</A><P>
</BODY>
</HTML>
```

The above left.html file will appear in the left window of the frameset. It contains two links that will change the contents of the right window, using the TARGET attribute, so display different pages relating to personal information.

Activity 6

Create the files frameset.html and left.html exactly as given above and save them with these names.

Load frameset.html into your browser and see the effects of frames. You might want to create more HTML files, and create links to them from left.html, in order to display then in the right frame window.

Web design

Introduction

Creating pages is one thing. Organizing information upon them in a logical manner and creating paths of links between pages is another quite different problem. Web design is a controversial field. There are no hard and fast answers. This section tries to present an approach to web design that synthesizes and simplifies a number of standard design approaches.

First, two vital definitions:

web page – contents of a window in a web browser

website – linked collection of web pages all serving one purpose (e.g. giving information about an organization).

Anyone can throw together a few web pages (for instance, for personal homepages). Websites are much more difficult for two reasons. First, they must incorporate a wide range of information about their subject. They may contain many hundreds of pages as a result and this raises the problem of how to organize links between all these pages. Second, websites must be fit for their purpose and serve the needs of their audience and users. This imposes constraints and demands on the website designers/maintainers. Therefore websites are the focus of this chapter, not web pages or 'home page' style sites.

Website design is about being able to structure information into web pages and then visualize simple navigation paths through those pages. One way of learning good website design is simply to look at other people's sites and conceptualize how they are structured. The purpose of this section is to propose and explain a checklist of features to use in appreciating good design from existing websites, so that new, effective websites can be designed.

Elements of website critique

The main headings under which a website can be critiqued are, in order of importance:

- content
- site structure and navigation
- graphic design and page layout
- technical issues
- web presence.

These headings are covered individually, with a general comment and then a listing of particular features to watch out for.

Content

Without content a website is useless. People will only use a website that gives them the information they need. If that information is not there they will go elsewhere. Features to check include:

- Is there an apparent audience for this website? If so, who are they? There might be a number of different types of user in the audience.
- Does the website meet audience needs? In the content the website provides, is anything missing, or is anything repeated? Does any material look to be out of date or incorrect?
- Is the language used on the website too technical or too informal? Are definitions of technical jargon given? Are there grammatical slips or spelling mistakes?
- On each page is there a meaningful title, content organized under appropriate headings and a clear statement of authorship and date of creation and last update?
- Is it possible to track how and when content was added to the website? Does it look as though the website could grow by adding new content over time?
- Are there warnings of unsuitable content (if necessary)?

Site structure and navigation

Content on a website must be findable by users. Content should be structured in a logical manner and links should guide a user through this content. The principle is to minimize effort on the part of the user in finding what they want. Features to check include:

- Is there a main page (gives headings for all the content on a website)? Is there a site map (a graphical representation of the website)? If one of these is present, how complete, clear and concise is it?
- Are main links labelled clearly and unambiguously (e.g. not using terms like 'miscellaneous', 'stuff' and 'reports')? Are text links clearly described (e.g. not using phrases like 'Click here'.) Are confusing icons without explanatory text used as links?
- Are there navigation aids (text and graphical navigation bars or windows giving a choice of links)? Are they used consistently in terms of their placement on the page and do they offer a sensible choice of links at all times? Is it possible to get back to the main page from any page on a website?
- Is the linking structure too 'deep' – does it take a lot of links to get from the main page to a chosen destination page? Can all content on a site be found from following no more than three links starting from the main page?
- Have standard browser navigation features been interfered with? The back button should always take a user back to the previous page they viewed and text link colours should not have been changed from the default (blue = unused, red = used).
- Is there a keyword search facility? Does it find useful answers to searches?

Graphic design and page layout

The aim is to give site an identity so that any page on a site is recognizable as belonging to that site. However, this identity should not be created by overuse of graphics or brash styles. Features to check include:

- Is there a consistency in the look and feel of pages? Do all pages share a common layout? Does this consistency give an interesting identity for the site?
- Has the need to scroll pages up and down and left and right been minimized?
- Have any pages been overloaded with text or graphics or both? Pages should almost never contain just text or graphics, there should always be a mixture.
- Have large, and/or garish, graphics been avoided? Are any graphics dull? Do all graphics serve a purpose?

Technical issues

There are a vast number of technological 'widgets' that can be used and using just those which add something to the site is the aim. However, just because a technology exists does not mean it has to be used. The prevalence in the late 1990s for sites to have front pages which load extravagant animations may have been aesthetically pleasing, but it served little purpose other than proving how clever the site designer was. Never assume a user possesses anything more than the most basic technology and a slow connection. Features to check include:

- Does the website overstep the mark by requiring a particular browser or browser version, plug-in (extra piece of software), window size or any other technical facility from the user?
- If the website includes files that are not viewable by a web browser (e.g. Word files), does it include links to sources of free software to view those files?
- Is the speed of page loading fast enough (does the site avoid using overlarge graphic files, complex pages, and so on)? Is a 'text only' version of the website available (as these can offset speed problems)?
- Do any pages contain broken links, missing graphics or generate browser errors?

Web presence

A website needs to be in portals and search engines on the internet if people are to know of its existence. It must state a privacy policy with regard to gathering data on users and it must give contact details (including standard address information). Features to check include:

- Is the website findable in major search engines/portals (e.g. Yahoo!, Dmoz, Altavista, Excite, Hotbot, Lycos, Google, etc.)?
- Does the website state its privacy policy?
- Does the website provide adequate contact information (address/telephone/fax) and an e-mail address for questions or comments?
- Has the website won any awards? Does it offer any usage statistics to show how popular it is?

Accessibility

Any web material should be accessible (in terms of readability) to the widest possible audience. There are two main issues here. One is that web pages must work for people who cannot see graphical content. The second is that not everyone understands English. The first issue can be tackled using the right tools and techniques. Multilingual web pages are much harder, as one needs to be able to translate content as and when it is produced into languages other than English. It is a human resource problem rather than a technical one.

There is specific pressure from the new Disability Discrimination Act to improve websites. Part 4 of the act makes it a requirement that public sector websites are accessible to all. This is not an onerous extra task as making a site accessible – this primarily means for the visually impaired – tends to be good for all users. A minimum requirement is to provide advice on accessibility, such as on increasing the size of type within a browser and to use ALT tags (textual alternatives to pictures and images that can be read out by a screen-reader).

For information on creating web pages accessible by those with visual disabilities see:

AbilityNet
www.abilitynet.org.uk/

RNIB: Web Access Centre
www.rnib.org.uk/xpedio/groups/public/documents/PublicWebsite/
public_webaccesscentre.hcsp

Web Accessibility Initiative: Getting Started: Making a Web Site Accessible
www.w3.org/WAI/gettingstarted/

Bobby (service that checks pages for compliance with some of the W3C guidelines.)
http://bobby.watchfire.com/

Activity 7

Choose one of the following websites:

The British Library
www.bl.uk/

Facet Publishing
www.facetpublishing.co.uk/index.shtml

Graduate School of Informatics, Strathclyde University
www.gsi.strath.ac.uk/gsi/

The People's Network
www.peoplesnetwork.gov.uk/

Using the preceding sections as a checklist, compile a critique of the chosen website.
How accessible is this website?

You might like to try the design critique checklist on your own organization's
website or a website that you like and compare the results with the website you
critiqued above.

Implementing web design

As was stated in the preceding section, website design is about being able to structure information into web pages and then visualize simple navigation paths
through those pages. The purpose of website critiquing is to develop skills in
looking at other people's sites and conceptualizing how they are structured. The
purpose of this section is to learn how to structure information on the web and
create sensible navigation paths that users find easy to follow. Whereas website
design critiquing is reactive, website design implementation skills are proactive,
enabling the creation of a new site rather than the examination of an existing one.
Software tools are not covered here. Tools can only serve someone who understands how to design. In themselves they give no help with the design process
whatsoever. Design is a conceptual process, not a mechanical one.

Two popular web authoring tools are Microsoft's Front Page and
Macromedia's Dreamweaver but there are many others, some of which are avail-
able as freeware. For a listing see: http://directory.google.com/Top/Computers/
Software/Internet/Authoring/HTML/WYSIWYG_Editors/.

Whatever tool you use, designing a website design breaks down into four
stages:

- identification of user groups
- content ordering and labelling
- structuring content
- enabling navigation.

Each of the above is dealt with individually in the following sections. Each section has an explanation followed by an example.

Identification of user groups

The audience for a website will be made of many distinct groups. Each group has particular needs, which must be met by the provision of certain content. Some needs, and thus content, might be shared by different groups. By far the best way of determining user needs is to ask users what they want. Failing the availability of users, a designer can create a table listing 'Audience' against 'Needs' and then 'Content required' to satisfy needs. Existing websites are a good source for determining user needs as the better ones will have been designed with user needs paramount. Table 5.1 shows how user needs might be identified for a website that sells toys.

Table 5.1   Table to determine user needs for a website selling toys

Audience	Needs	Content required
Children	Fun	Lively toy descriptions, pictures, animations
	Trendiness	Reviews/ratings by children, showcase for new toys
	Serendipity	A variety of routes (brand, character, type) to toys
Parents	Value	Discount schemes, special offers
	Suitability	Details of toy durability and safety, reviews and ratings by parents
	Fast service	Quick, responsive purchasing system
Relatives	Gift ideas	Best selling toys, by age group
	Gift shipment	Wrapping and special delivery services
	Fast service	[as for Parents above]

Activity 8

Complete an 'Audience – Needs – Content required' table for a website for your organization or for a domain or topic you are interested in. Always take the point of view of external users, not insiders. For example, just because an organization has an accounts department does not mean that users of that organization will want to know of its existence. They might want to know about the facilities it provides, however.

Content ordering and labelling

Content ordering is concerned with how individual pieces of content are to be grouped together. Some sort of logical ordering is needed. There are two basic ways of approaching content, each requiring different ordering schemes:

- when users know exactly what they want ('known item search')
- when users have only a vague feeling about what they want ('browse search').

Known item searches are best aided by alphabetical, chronological, numeric or geographical orderings. Browse searches conversely are best supported by subject, topic, type or task-oriented orderings. The latter are the hardest orderings to construct as all members of a subject, topic, type or task must be explicitly defined. Consult dictionaries and thesauri to derive complete lists of members. Care must be taken to label each member as clearly and unambiguously as possible. Labels should be consistent, for example by using plural forms where possible.

Most websites will be hybrid, containing mixtures of orderings. For example, using the data provided in Table 5.1, content ordering would identify toys using a known item search by:

- brand name (e.g. Lego, Meccano, Scalextric, Tomy or Brio)
- character (e.g. Pokemon, Thomas the Tank Engine, Barbie or Action Man).

It would identify toys using a browse search by:

- type (e.g. dolls, action figures, soft toys, construction kits, jigsaws, board games, magic sets, musical instruments, model vehicles or sports equipment)
- age group
- release date
- bestsellers
- special offer price.

Activity 9

Derive 'known item search' and 'browse search' orderings for the example you chose in Activity 8. Do your best at constructing complete member lists for subject, type and topic orders.

Structuring content

Once content orderings are known, it is possible to derive a web structure from them. Most websites have hierarchical structures, starting from a main/home/index/top page. From this page there should be a limited number of choices (a maximum of seven from user studies), which lead down to pages on the second level of the hierarchy. These choices should match the first level orderings, and so on down from the second level.

If there are too many first level orderings then the main/home/index/top page could contain choices relating to type of user instead.

Beware of too deep a hierarchy. A maximum of three levels is good. It may not be possible to keep a three level hierarchy and give users no more than seven choices at each level. In this situation, increase choices to avoid deepening the hierarchy. Some sites such as Yahoo! present large numbers of choices on the main/home/index/top page to avoid deep hierarchies. For example, based on the above user data for a toy website, using content organization above produces:

LEVEL 1

Main page Links: brand name, character, type, age, release date, sales, special offers

LEVEL 2

Brand name page Links: Lego, Meccano, Scalextric, Tomy, Brio, etc.

Character page Links: Pokemon, Thomas the Tank Engine, Barbie, Action Man, etc.

Type page Links: dolls, action figures, soft toys, construction kits, jigsaws, board games, magic sets, musical instruments, model vehicles, sports equipment, etc.

Age group page Links: < 1, 1–3, 4–5, 6–8, 9–11, 12 >

Release date page Links: today, this week, last week, this month, last month

Best sellers page Links: brand name, character, type, age group

Special offers page Links: details of individual toys on special offer

LEVEL 3

[NB not all level 3 pages shown, just one example for each level 2 page.]

Lego page Links: individual Lego sets

Pokemon page Links: Pokemon card sets

Dolls page Links: Barbie, Cindy etc.

< 1 page Links: Baby toys

Today page Links: new toys out today (if any)

Best sellers by brand name page Links: best selling Lego toys etc.

Activity 10

Derive a hierarchy from the 'known item search' and 'browse search' organizations for the material you produced in Activity 9. Try and complete it at least to the second level and have some third level pages.

Enabling navigation

Navigation enables a user to plan a route, to determine their current location and to be able to move up and down the hierarchy, as well as follow related paths between different sections of the hierarchy. Once content ordering has been done, and a hierarchy derived from them, navigation aids can be produced. Navigation aids consist of a list of links that can be presented to the user in a variety of ways (as a list, a menu, a frame, and so on).

From each page produced by the hierarchy design, navigation links are needed back to the main/home/index/top page and to the appropriate page(s) at the level(s) above. The names of links should match the names of the pages to which they lead. Page names should be based on the labels used in orderings. A good navigation aid will also point to related pages in the hierarchy (if any). Identifying these related pages is hard and there is no easy, automatic method.

Some websites use devices like a table of contents page, an index page (like a book index), a site map (a picture of the hierarchy) or a guided tour as extra navigation aids.

It is vital to test any prototype website on representative users from groups identified in 1 above. For example, two possibilities are given below from the orderings and structure derived previously:

LEVEL 3
Lego page Links: individual Lego toys
Standard navigation links: main page, Level 2 brand name page
Related page links:
Level 3 best sellers by brand name Lego page
Level 3 construction kits page

LEVEL 3
< 1 page Links: baby toys
Standard navigation links: main page, Level 2 age groups page
Related page links:
Level 3 soft toys page
Level 3 educational toys page
Level 3 best sellers by age groups, < 1 page

Activity 11

Pick pages from your hierarchy produced in Activity 10 at levels 2 and 3 and try and find one or more related pages for them.

Web page layout

Now we have learned how to design a website, and how to work out content and links (in theory) for all the pages on a site, we need to look in detail at how to lay out individual web pages. The problem here is that HTML was never designed to lay out text and associated images, in the ways we are accustomed to seeing in printed media, but rather just to display text and graphics in a simple manner appropriate for a wide range of computer displays. Thus HTML has to be pressed into service when used for layout purposes.

Tables

Tables can be a powerful way of laying out content on web pages. Tables enable vertical and horizontal structure to a page especially when table borders are made invisible. Pick a website and the chances are that if you view the HTML source of the home page of that website you will see a table being used for formatting. You should already know how to create basic tables using HTML tags. Extra tags you need to use tables in page formatting are given in the examples below.

Example 1

```
<table border="0" width="100%" cellpadding="10"
cellspacing="0">
<tr>
<td width="75%" align="center" bgcolor="red">
This is column one.
</td>
<td width="25%" align="right" bgcolor="blue">
This is column two.
</td>
</tr>
</table>
```

In the example above, table border value 0 (zero) hides borders. The width value of 100% for a table makes a table fill the available browser screen; resizing the browser will automatically resize the table and preserve formatting. Cells will automatically be spaced proportionally to their number (for example two cells will each take up 50% of a row). However, this can be overridden by width values for cells (for instance 75%/25% for two cells in a row). Cellpadding simply creates a gap between content and the side of a cell. This is advisable to create 'white space' to keep text easy to read. Cellspacing creates white space between cells: this is not needed. Bgcolor (and background to link to an image file) can be used to set colours and images as backgrounds for cells. Align values for content for each cell can be left, right, center (note American spelling), top or bottom. Another example follows:

Example 2

```
<table width="100%" border="1" cellspacing="0" cell-
padding="1" height="500">
<tr>
<td colspan="2" height="100"> </td>
</tr>
<tr>
<td> </td>
<td rowspan="2"> </td>
</tr>
<tr>
<td> </td>
</tr>
</table>
```

Tables can also have a height value in pixels, as set in Example 2. Cells are given heights proportional to their number in a column (for instance two cells in a column would each take up 50% of the table height value). Cells can also be given height values to override this default proportionality. Empty cells are made by using a non-breaking space character to give the empty cell 'content' that is invisible (without content the cell would not display at all). Special characters are preceded by '&' and end with ';' and 'nbsp' indicates non-breaking space. Colspan (and rowspan) are used to merge successive cells in the same column (and row).

Activity 12

Have a look at the tables the above HTML code produces in your browser.

Create a web front page for an online newspaper (see Figure 5.1). The first row should run across the top of the page, and will contain the newspaper's title with an appropriate image as a background. This row should not be that deep. Centre align material in this row (and left align all subsequent material). The first column should run to the bottom of the page and will contain the contents for the newspaper (e.g. links to succeeding pages). The next two columns will contain the lead story: an appropriate image should be used to run across the top of these two columns. Add enough dummy text so the page looks realistic. Make the backgrounds of the contents and lead story columns different colours. (HINT: start with a three by three regular empty table first, and then change it bit by bit into the newspaper page, see Figure 5.1).

Newspaper title		
Contents column	Lead story picture	
.....		
	Lead story column	Lead story column continues .....

Figure 5.1 Simple table used to create a web front page for an online newspaper

You might try to add a lead story title running across the two lead story columns, under the picture.

Using cascading style sheets for formatting

As well as controlling where text and images appears, we also need to be able to change the appearance of text from the standard font that a browser imposes. The best way of handling fonts is to use cascading style sheets (CSS). Style sheets are a facility in HTML that allows fonts, colours, margins, alignments and more to be set for existing HTML tags and user-defined extensions to tags. Note that some (older) browsers cannot handle style sheets. Any instructions in a style sheet that a browser cannot handle (for instance unusual font type) will be ignored and the standard default used instead.

The following example shows how to use a style sheet:

```
<HTML>
<HEAD>
<TITLE>CSS example</TITLE>
<STYLE TYPE="text/css">
```

```
H1 {font-family: Arial; font-style: italic; font-
size: 48; color: #00ff00; text-align: center;}
P {color: yellow; font-size: 20}

</STYLE>
</HEAD>

<BODY>
<H1>A green Arial font 48pt italic centred
header</H1>
<P>Yellow 20pt text, Mary had a little lamb, testing
testing, 1, 2, 3
etc.</P>
</BODY>
</HTML>
```

First, note the style sheet declaration – 'text/css' denotes a style sheet that follows the CSS standard. This declaration is enclosed in STYLE tags and comes in the HEAD part of an HTML document. After the tags BODY, H1 and P comes a style sheet – a list of style declarations. These ought to be self-explanatory. Note that any BODY style sheet declarations will apply to content in H1 and P tags, since these are part of the BODY.

Styles can also be defined for user-defined classes of existing tags. For example, the paragraph (P) tag can have classes first, last, important, bold, italic and so on, and each of these can have a style sheet to give it the required properties. Note that the style sheet for the parent tag (in this case P) is used and modified by the extra or different properties in the class style sheet. See the following example:

```
<HTML>
<HEAD>
<TITLE>CSS example 1</TITLE>
<STYLE TYPE="text/css">

H1 {font-family: Arial; font-style: italic; font-
size: 48; color: #00ff00; text-align: center;}
P {color: yellow; font-size: 20}
P.first {color:blue; }
```

```
</STYLE>
</HEAD>

<BODY>
<H1>A green Arial font 48pt italic centred
header</H1>
<P CLASS="first">This is a blue text first paragraph.
Otherwise it is the same as following
paragraph.</P>
<P>Yellow 20pt text, Mary had a little lamb, testing
testing, 1, 2, 3
etc.</P>
</BODY>
</HTML>
```

A problem with internal style sheets – style sheet declarations contained within a page – is that if we wish to change a style property then we have to edit every page containing that style property. The solution is to use an external style – have our style properties in a file external to the page itself – and reference this external style sheet from the page. Thus changing one style property in an external style sheet will change that property in every page that references that style sheet. Note that styles defined internally to a page will override definitions in external style sheets, hence the name 'cascading' style sheets, in which documents inherit a basic style but can impose changes if they wish.

This is an external style sheet file called mystyles.css. It contains the styles previously used internally:

```
<STYLE TYPE="text/css">

H1 {font-family: Arial; font-style: italic; font-
size: 48; color: #00ff00; text-align: center;}
P {color: yellow; font-size: 20;}
P.first {color:blue; }

</STYLE>
```

This is our main HTML page, now containing a reference to the above external style sheet:

```
<HTML>
<HEAD>
<TITLE>CSS example 2</TITLE>

<LINK REL="stylesheet" TYPE="text/css"
HREF="mystyles.css">

</HEAD>

<BODY>
<H1>A green Arial font 48pt italic centred
header</H1>
<P CLASS="first">This is a blue text first paragraph.
Otherwise it is the same as following
paragraph.</P>
<P>Yellow 20pt text, Mary had a little lamb, testing
testing, 1, 2, 3
etc.</P>
</BODY>
</HTML>
```

Activity 13

Imagine that the newspaper whose layout you created earlier wishes to use an external style sheet to control the appearance of text on its pages. Create a file newspaper.css with different styles for text in the different sections of the main page. Also have a style for the initial paragraph of the lead story.

Client-side programming

Tables and stylesheets are very basic ways of controlling web page layout. There are much more sophisticated ways using layers (essentially overlapping tables) and Dynamic HTML, controlling HTML with programming code. This is known as client-side programming, using programming languages like JavaScript and Java (these are not similar despite having similar names). These programs run within the browser on the client's machine. The client-side program has to be downloaded, along with its containing web page, and this can be a disadvantage in terms of extra data to transfer. The pay-off is in greater flexibility, and even interactivity, in web pages. Once you have mastered tables and style sheets, then client-side programming are worth exploring.

JavaScript

The following is an example of a simple JavaScript program:

```
<html>
<body>
<form>
<input type="button" value = "Click Here" onClick =
"alert('You clicked')">
</form>
</body>
</html>
```

When loaded and run in a browser, this code will produce a button on the screen labelled 'Click Here'. When this button is clicked on, the 'onClick' alert is triggered and creates an alert box.

It is possible to get JavaScript to recognize mouse movements as well as mouse clicks, as the following code illustrates:

```
<a href="#" onMouseOver="myimage.src = 'image2.gif';
return true">
<img src = "image1.gif" NAME = "myimage">
</a>
```

The line that starts <img src tells the computer to put an image called 'myimage' on the screen. It finds this image in the file 'image1.gif'. The line that starts <a href= tells the computer that when the mouse moves over the image (onMouseOver), it is to replace it with the image in file image2.gif.

As was mentioned above, JavaScript can do more than just react to input, as the following example illustrates:

```
<html>
<body>
<script language = "JavaScript">
document.write("<h2>Table of Factorials</h2>");
for (i = 1, fact = 1; i < 10; i++, fact =fact* i ) {
    document.write( i + "! =" + fact );
    document.write("<br>");
}
```

```
</script>
</body>
</html>
```

It is a simple computer program. `Fact` and `i` are variables; they contain numbers. "fact = fact * i" means multiply `fact` by `i` and put this value back into `fact`. The line "for (i=1," etc. tells the computer to go round in a loop. "i++" means add one on to `i` each time we go round the loop. The two brackets { and } show the start and end of this loop. Everything between these brackets is repeated 9 times. (From i =1 to i = 9, when i < 10.)

"document.write" is how JavaScript tells the web browser to write something to the web page (the document). In this example the JavaScript tells the web browser to write "<br>" to the web page. The JavaScript also tells the web browser to display the value of "i", the exclamation mark and equals signs, and then the value of "fact".

The previous examples demonstrate merely a handful of JavaScript features. If you are interested in learning how to write your own JavaScripts visit the link below for tutorials and guides to JavaScript: http://dmoz.org/Computers/ Programming/Languages/JavaScript/Tutorials/.

For a complete description of JavaScript see the Reference Manual at http://developer.netscape.com/docs/manuals/communicator/jsguide4/index.htm.

If you are not interested in JavaScript programming, you can download (and amend if necessary) already written JavaScript programs from online libraries and use them in your web pages. The best is The JavaScript Source at http://javascript.internet.com/.

Activity 13

IMPORTANT: you must type in the example programs above with all the punctuation exactly as it is otherwise they will not work correctly!

In the first code example, which produces an alert box, try changing the 'value' of the button prompt to some other appropriate command. Change the 'alert' so it fits in with the new 'value'.

In the second code example, go to www.iconbizaar.com/ and choose two related images to save as image1.gif (or jpg) and image2.gif (or jpg) in your web page directory. Add the line below beginning `onMouseOut` to the second code example above in the appropriate place and remove `>` from the end of the preceding line:

```
<a href="#" onMouseOver="myimage.src = `image2.gif`;
```

```
return true;"
onMouseOut = "myimage.src='image1.gif'; return true;" >
<img src = "image1.gif" NAME = "myimage">
</a>
```

Move your mouse on and off the image to see what happens.

Alter the final JavaScript code example, so that, instead of multiplying each number, it adds each number. Then alter the JavaScript code so it so that it starts with 9 and works its way down to 1.

What if we want the factorial list to be created only when we push a button or click on an image? We can put the factorial calculator into a simple function. Enter the following HTML and JavaScript code:

```
<html>
<body>
<script language = "JavaScript">
function factorials () {
document.write("<h2>Table of Factorials</h2>");
for (i = 1, fact = 1; i < 10; i++, fact = fact * i ) {
document.write( i + "! =" + fact );
document.write("<br>");
}
return false;
}
</script>
<a href="#" onMouseOver= "factorials(); return
false;" >
<img src='image1.gif'>
</a>
</body>
</html>
```

A function is where we group things together to do one job. With JavaScript we 'call the function'. Now change the function so that it is called 'adds' and make it produce the list of additions you created previously. If you feel confident, put both 'factorials' and 'adds' onto the same web-page and allow the user to click on a different image for each. Alter the JavaScript program so that it uses buttons.

Java

The Java language was developed by Sun Microsystems almost by accident. In the early 1990s (before the world wide web) Sun developed a language called Oak that was capable of networking all electronic devices within a home (such as garage doors, toasters and refrigerators). This language was platform independent (which meant it could run on any operating system). The networking project was dropped; however, Sun saw a use for the language on the internet. In 1995 the Oak language was modified and renamed Java. Sun then released a product called HotJava that could run programs written in the Java language. Since then Java has been incorporated directly into browsers.

Programmers write programs in Java using some type of Java development software. Once the program is written, they will compile or link it. It is the compiled or linked version of the program that produces an applet. Note that applets do not contain readable Java code, rather executable code. Applet files have a .class extension to identify them. The Java language itself is quite complex, so non-programmers will find it very difficult to create applets. However, because it is complex, it is far more powerful than JavaScript.

When a user requests a web page containing a Java applet, the applet is downloaded, along with the page, to the user's computer. Because the applet and page are downloaded from the internet and run from the user's computer, they are called client-side programs. When an applet is run, it opens a window. If the applet is embedded in the page, the window appears directly on the web page. If you have a link to the applet, a separate window will open and run the applet.

You can download many free Java applets on the world wide web. There are clocks, calculators, spreadsheets, search tools and many others. The best place to get Java applets is at http://javaboutique.internet.com/.

Note that most Java applets are stored compressed. You will need to uncompress them before using them. Some of the Java applets on the web come with source code – the readable version of Java applets. Programming Java involves writing programs in Java source code and then compiling these programs into Java applet form. There are free programming tools (Java development kits) available for Java programming. For tutorials on programming in Java and tools available see http://dmoz.org/Computers/Programming/Languages/Java/.

Activity 14

IMPORTANT: you must type in the example that follows exactly as it is otherwise things may not work correctly!

Go to http://javaboutique.internet.com/Corf_Scroller/, download and unzip the file corf_scroller.class, and save it to your HTML file . In a text editor like Notepad Notepad create the following HTML file and view it in a browser:

```
<html>
<head>
<title>Scroller applet</title>
</head>
<body>
<APPLET code="Corf_Scroller.class" width="500"
height="50" vspace="50" hspace="50">
<PARAM NAME="Corf_Timer" VALUE="8">
<PARAM NAME="Corf_Link"
VALUE="www.dis.strath.ac.uk/courses/ts/java/">
<PARAM NAME="Corf_Target" VALUE="_new">
<PARAM NAME="Corf_Text" VALUE=" My first Java applet ">
<PARAM NAME="Corf_ForeGround" VALUE="CC3333">
<PARAM NAME="Corf_Thickness" VALUE="2">
<PARAM NAME="Corf_Font" VALUE="TimesRoman">
</APPLET>
</body>
</html>
```

The <applet> tags allow applets to be embedded in HTML. After 'code' above comes the name of the Java applet file. The standard values width, height, vspace and hspace above are all changeable. Experiment by giving them new values to see what happens. The parameters that follow are fed into the applet itself. Again try changing them to see what they do. What happens when you click on the scroller? The operations of any applet can be controlled by changing its parameters.

To verify that Java applets are indeed not readable try opening Corf_Scroller.class in a text editor, like Notepad.

Server-side programming

In previous sections we have looked at static web pages. In a static web page, the HTML and the content of the page have to be created in advance and then stored on a web server. When a user via their browser requests that web page, a copy is sent as is. The user can only view the page and cannot alter it in any way. Thus it is said to be 'static', as its content is fixed and determined before viewing and cannot be changed by the user during or after viewing.

Dynamic web pages are created only when requested by a browser. Essentially a program or an application on a web server creates a page by wrapping content in appropriate HTML tags. Activating program code on the web server is called server-side scripting. The program code does its job and passes the results back to the web server in the form of a web page, which the web server returns to the browser on the client's machine. Server-side scripting technologies are vital in integrating web servers and web technology with other software applications and information resources. There are disadvantages to server-side scripting. For example, they are adversely affected by slow network speeds between the user and the server and by overloading of the server itself.

Just as with client-side programming, there are a variety of available technologies. All web servers come with a special Common Gateway Interface (CGI) capability, which essentially involves the ability to run a program in a directory visible to the web server, normally called the 'cgi-bin' directory. Special programming languages like PERL and PHP are used to create CGI programs. These languages tend to be open standard, like Java. A version of Java, Java servlets, can also be used for server-side scripting.

Proprietary technologies are also available, either as extensions to a web server which allow server-side scripting, like Active Server Pages (ASP) from Microsoft or as middleware, applications that link a web server with another application, like a database.

Active Server Page scripting

An example of an ASP file is:

```
<%@ language="javascript" %>
<html>
<head>
<title>
First Active Server Page
</title>
</head>
<body>
<%
Response.Write("Hello World!")
%>
```

```
</body>
</html>
```

The `<%..%>` delimiters contain a simple script which writes an HTML page. The language command warns the ASP engine that it must deal with JavaScript while `Response.Write` is a JavaScript command. The rest of the file is standard HTML.

When a browser requests the above file, for example by using http://name.of.server/example.asp, the ASP engine on the server executes the script and outputs any results in HTML. The requesting browser only sees HTML. Thus ASP scripts in files stored on ASP-aware servers are never visible to users. ASP scripts can be used to change web page content dynamically, respond to input from users and access other data and resources and return the results as web pages.

Forms

To enable user input into a server-side application, a form is used. Forms can be defined using standard HTML tags. Form elements are elements that allow the user to enter information (like text fields, textarea fields, drop-down menus, radio buttons, checkboxes, etc.) in a form.

Here is an example form showing, respectively, text boxes, radio buttons and check boxes:

```
<html>
<head>
<title>
First form
</title>
</head>
<body>
<h1>Form to record student details</h1>
<form name="submit"
action="http://[servername]/[filename].asp"
method="get">
First name:
<input type="text" name="firstname">
<br>
Last name:
```

```
<input type="text" name="lastname">
<P>
<input type="radio" name="sex" value="male"> Male
<input type="radio" name="sex" value="female"> Female
<P>
<P>
Age: <select name="agelist">
<option value="age1"><21</option>
<option value="age2">21-29</option>
<option value="age3">30-39</option>
<option value="age4">>39</option>
</select>
<P>
Course: <input type="checkbox" name="IM"
value="yes">IM
<input type="checkbox" name="ILS" value="yes">ILS
<P>
<input type="submit" value="Submit">
</form>
</body>
</html>
```

Text boxes, radio buttons and check boxes are all 'input types' with 'names', whose purpose is to label the input type. Radio buttons and check boxes have 'values', which are returned to the server, while text boxes return whatever text is entered into them. 'Select' creates a drop-down menu with items each with a differing value.

The whole form has a 'name' (DISinput), which like input type names is to label this form. 'Method', however, is vital as it decides how data is sent from the form to the server. 'Get' sends data in the clear – as the trailing part of a URL. There is an alternative method, called 'Post', which sends data hidden to the server. Clicking on the 'Submit' button sends the form contents to the server. Finally there is an 'Action' – the name and server location of the ASP file, which is activated to process returned data.

Activity 15

Enter the example form given above, save it as form.html and view it in a browser. What happens after you fill in the form and then click on the Submit button? Try changing the method from get to post and again fill in and submit the form. What is different?

Linking Active Server Pages, forms and databases

The linking element between forms and ASP pages is a method of passing the values of named form elements to ASP scripts. ASP scripts, as well as dealing with input from forms and producing web pages, can also deal with applications like databases. Thus, imagine a simple database of books. A form could be set up to enable a user to search the book database and request a book. ASP scripts would allow the user to search the database, via commands entered by a form, and would also use a form to allow books to be requested. Finally the ASP script could add data to the database to reserve requested books so that subsequent users who request them are told a book is not available.

The link between forms, server-side scripting and databases is vitally important in delivering content over the web. Most large, well used websites store content in a database and extract that content on demand by server-side scripting to deliver pages to browsers. If you want to be serious about web publishing, you must eschew static pages and embrace some form of dynamic page delivery from a database of content.

XML and XSL

XML (Extensible Markup Language)

HTML provides a set of tags which enable data display. XML provides a method of defining sets of tags that describe and structure data, but do not display it. Display is handled by style sheets.

Rather than learning tags, which one has to do to use HTML, with XML one must learn how to define tags. All tags must be self-describing – their names must describe the content they will contain. Tags must come in pairs. A pair of tags and their content is known as an element. Tag names can be in upper and lower case but the names in tag pairs must match, character for character and case for case. Different tag pairs may not overlap. All XML documents must follow these rules to be valid (also known as 'well formed'). See the following as an example:

```
<book>
    <title>Macbeth</title>
    <author>
                <forename>William</forename>
                <surname>Shakespeare</surname>
    </author>
</book>
```

The indentation above is not needed by XML but is used to make clear the tagging structure (also known as the document tree). The 'book' tag is the root element of the document tree, as all other tags are enclosed by it. 'Book' is also the parent of 'author' and 'title', as these tags are nested directly inside it. These two tags can also be described as the element content of 'book'. Conversely, 'author' and 'title' can be said to be children (or siblings) of 'book'. This nesting of tags can continue indefinitely: 'author' is the parent of 'forename' and 'surname', and they are its siblings. Since 'forename' and 'surname' have no sibling tags, they only have textual data as children, and are said to have simple content.

To label the above as an XML document an initial declaration is needed:

```
<?xml version="1.0"?>
```

An alternative to using child elements to link data to an element, attributes can be used. An attribute is a name or value pair associated with an element. For example, to add a format to a publisher tag one can use:

```
<publisher format="paperback">Smith and Son</publisher>
```

instead of:

```
<publisher>
    <name>Smith and Son</name>
    <format>paperback</format>
</publisher>
```

Your browser gives a rather plain view of XML. Cascading Style Sheets (CSSs) are used to control the display of XML documents. The use of CSS with XML is identical to that with HTML. For example:

```
book {display: block}
title {font-size:24pt; color: red}
author {font-size:16pt}
forename {color: blue}
surname {color: black}
```

will apply styles to the example given above. Note that the first style declaration (display: block) causes all the siblings of the book tag to appear on one line in the display. Also note that styles given to parent tags (author) are inherited by sibling tags. Attributes are dealt with by replacing 'attribute' by 'class' in the XML file and assigning styles in the external style sheet to particular content items, for example:

```
publisher.paperback {color: yellow}
```

Like an HTML file, an XML file needs a reference to the external style sheet:

```
<?xml-stylesheet type="text/css" href="style.css"?>
```

where style.css is the name of the external style sheet.

Activity 16

Create in Notepad an XML document for a list of books for either a library or a bookshop. Books should be identifiable by author, title and publisher. Enter at least six books.

Save your XML document as books.xml and view it in Internet Explorer. If it views with errors fix them and reload the XML document. What do you see? What does clicking on the '+' and '-' signs do?

If the XML document viewed without errors, change the case of one letter in one tag, save it and view it again. You should get an error message.

Create in Notepad an external style sheet for your XML document books.xml, that you created in the previous activity. View the XML document in Internet Explorer. Try experimenting by changing style definitions in the style sheet and reloading books.xml in your browser.

XSL (Extensible Style Sheet Language)

Cascading Style Sheets cannot process the data within elements in any way, only display that data. XSL can allocate styles to data within an element and process that data, for instance when it detects a particular element and data it can do things with that data, for example store it in a database. XSL is more of a programming language than a style sheet definition tool.

An example of a simple XSL style sheet follows:

```
<?xml version="1.0"?>
<xsl:stylesheet version="1.0"
xmlns:xsl="www.w3.org/TR/WD-xsl">
<xsl:template match="/">
<html>
<head>
<title>A Simple XSL style sheet</title>
</head>
<body>
<xsl:for-each select="library/book">
<p>
<xsl:value-of select="." />
</p>
</xsl:for-each>
</body>
</html>
</xsl:template>
</xsl:stylesheet>
```

The above example starts with an XML declaration as XSL tags are defined in XML. The xmlns declaration defines a 'namespace' to use in interpreting XSL tags. This namespace is the XML declaration of what tags are allowed. Note that the above namespace has been superseded but Internet Explorer uses it as its XSL namespace.

The template tag above with the value match="/" tells XSL to begin working at the root element of the XML document it will process. The for-each tag creates a loop which works through each sibling element (book) of the XML document root element (library). The value-of tag with select="." means display all elements of each root sibling. Note the use of the self-closing value-of tag (the final '/').

To display sibling elements and attributes respectively the select statement needs to be modified as below:

```
<xsl:value-of select="author/forename" />
<xsl:value-of select="publisher/@format" />
```

It appears as though HTML tags are being used to format output as a web page but actually XHTML is being used. XHTML is an application of XML and is an XML definition of the allowable tags in HTML and how they can be nested. XHTML requires that all HTML tags be used in pairs (although single empty tags, e.g. </ p>, are permitted), that all tags names are in lower case and that tags are not nested illegally inside other tags. XHTML is the successor to the final HTML standard, 4.0.

To reference an XSL style sheet the following is used:

```
<?xml-stylesheet type="text/xsl" href="style.xsl"?>
```

where style.xsl is the name of the XSL style sheet file in the same directory as the referencing XML file. Note the use of 'xsl' as the extension denoting XSL style sheets.

Two more facilities of XSL need to be explained. First, how are actual style declarations (for colour, font and so on) made? Second, in the introduction to XSL it was stated that XSL can process data from XML documents and not merely display it. An example that covers both is a simple 'if' statement, for example if format='paperback' then apply a style to the current XHTML tag:

```
<p>
<xsl:if test=".[publisher/@format='paperback']">
<xsl:attribute
name="style">color:green</xsl:attribute>
</xsl:if>
<xsl:value-of select="." />
</p>
```

If the format is a paperback then the P tag will be set to green so all the output for the value-of tag will be in green. Instead of changing the attribute value, the 'if' statement could open a database and copy the output from the value-of tag there. Note that for the 'if' statement to be triggered, the sought data in the test must match, character for character and case for case, with the data from the XML document. Note also that the '@' character indicates an attribute of an element. Elements themselves are separated by just '/'.

Activity 17

Create in Notepad an external XSL style sheet for your XML document books.xml, which you created in a previous activity. View the XML document in Internet Explorer. Display only selected elements and attributes, rather than all of them. By using XHTML tags, make your XML content appear in a table.

Experiment on your external XSL style sheet, which you created in a previous activity.

Make all books by one author appear in a different colour.

Using XML

We have already seen one application of XML, namely XHTML. There are many more. Two examples have been chosen. Each essentially involves defining a set of tags in XML for use with a particular application, and saving that master set of tags as a Document Type Declaration (DTD), also known as an XML Schema.

WML (Wireless Markup Language) is an XML-defined tagging language for displaying data on mobile phone screens. WML was designed for use with Wireless Access Protocol (WAP) mobile phones. WML makes sure that content is displayed in a way appropriate for the small screen of mobile phones.

Metadata is data about data. Metadata is used to describe and summarize the content of web pages and related information, for example, who authored the page. Search engines can use such information to retrieve pages. Resource Description Format (RDF) is a set of XML tags, again defined in a DTD, for holding metadata. Since there are various standards for recording different metadata, RDF can accommodate these standards.

XML is a vast and ever growing field. New schemas are appearing for new domains all the time. The main repository is at www.w3c.org/XML/, but there are good sites at www.xml.com/ and www.xml.org/.

Activity 18

In your browser go to www.gelon.net.

This site is a 'wapaliser' – it converts pages in WAP (WML) format to be displayed on a web page, using the device of a mobile phone image to display them. Into the wapaliser box enter http://wap.tees.ac.uk/ and experiment by using the 'phone' controls. Now view this page in Internet Explorer. The browser will fail to recognize it as browsers cannot read WML, only HTML and basic XML. Save the page to disk as waptees.xml and then try to view this page in your browser. It should work: why? Find some tags used in WML that you have not seen in HTML. Can you work out what they do? HINT: look at the original page again in the wapaliser. Find the address of the DTD used to define the tags in WML.

In your browser go to www.strath.ac.uk and view the page source. At the page header you will see HTML ' meta name' tags giving information about the University home page. Who created this page?

In your browser go to www.ukoln.ac.uk/metadata/dcdot/.

This page will automatically generate RDF and Dublin Core metadata. Enter the URL of the Strathclyde University home page (www.strath.ac.uk), check the Display as RDF box and click on Submit. Copy the resulting data, paste it into Notepad and save it as strath.xml. View this file in Internet Explorer.

There are two namespaces defined, one for RDF and one for Dublin Core (DC). Find the addresses of these. Find examples of RDF and DC tags. Note that all the DC tags are nested inside one RDF tag, 'description'.

Reference

Poulter, A., Hiom, D. and McMenemy, D. (2005) *The Library and Information Professional's Internet Companion*, London, Facet Publishing.

6 Creating simple portal solutions in public libraries

David McMenemy, Margaret Houston and Liz McGettigan

Introduction

While in her term as the first President of CILIP, Sheila Corrall stated that:

> Information and communications technologies have made information superficially much easier to access but actually much harder to assess – in terms of its accuracy, provenance, reliability. Knowledge and information professionals are essential in guiding users to timely, accurate, quality information, and to helping them gain skills to find this for themselves.
> (CILIP, 2002, 6)

One of the main ways information workers have been providing this guidance has been through the creation of entry points to the information, which in the electronic world are sometimes referred to as portals. Rather then decreasing the need for such solutions, the electronic world has exacerbated the need for quality entry points to information, and the role of the community librarian in that duty has never been more important. This chapter, then, has three main objectives:

- to define the portal concept in terms of its relevance to community libraries and learning centres
- to examine successful implementations of the portal concept in community settings

- to suggest potential scenarios for implementing simple digital solutions in a local setting using easily available pre-existing tools.

What are portals?

The basic definition of what a portal represents is an obvious one – an entrance or gateway to something beyond; that something is normally highly valued by the seeker. A community library or learning centre itself can be defined as a portal to the wealth of knowledge accessible therein, not merely in its collection of materials but in the knowledge and skills of its staff. In one context the training undertaken by public library staff as a result of People's Network funding enables users to enter a portal to new skills development when they visit their public library. Indeed, community libraries themselves have always been information portals for the users in their areas, to a wealth of information on the local community and beyond. As O'Leary states, 'portals are new in name only . . . . The role of information clearinghouse has long been performed by libraries' (O'Leary, 2000, 38).

In the modern era, however, the term portal is increasingly becoming associated with electronic gateways rather than physical gateways. For instance, Zhou has accurately deemed the term portal to be 'one of the buzzwords of the networked age' (Zhou, 2003, 120). In the world of information, 'portals are . . . important tools to facilitate the hard task of finding and accessing useful information' (Pinto and Fraser, 2003). There should be a concern, then, that as users justifiably begin to expect such electronic solutions to be available for all of their information needs, that the wealth of resources available in community libraries may become under-used. Additionally, the concern for information workers must be that as users continue to view the potential electronic solution as the solution of choice, they are in effect supplying themselves with improper or incomplete information using library resources. As Debowski has stated:

> In the past, information workers had a keen understanding of their user population. This was developed through regular on-site interactions. Users were assisted to find information, and their search behaviours were monitored to check for any difficulties. The individual idiosyncrasies of patrons were readily identifiable and catered for.
>
> (Debowski, 2000, 175)

Local solutions continue to be absolutely vital for the information needs of customers. While large-scale projects, such as the types that will be discussed below, can offer excellent gateways to important information, there remains a need for low-level solutions to bespoke information problems, and for the information skills of public library staff to be nurtured and developed through the creation of resources to solve these problems. As Arnold has stated, 'knowing what is out there, and how to access it has been one of the librarian's much underrated skills. As has our ability to evaluate and analyse a source for it quality' (Arnold, 2001, 180).

To this end, this chapter argues that simple digital portals can be relatively easily introduced in local libraries to enhance user enquiries and community information needs, even in a stand-alone fashion. While many authorities are introducing robust e-government solutions (see Chapter 4), there is a danger that such approaches can be led by local authority priorities rather than user priorities, and as such that much of the wealth of information that community libraries normally provide to their local communities may be in danger of being marginalized.

Building on the ICT training they have received both in the workplace and in the earlier chapters of this book, staff in community libraries and learning centres can produce straightforward web-enhanced portals using simple techniques learned from the activities at the end of this chapter. These techniques require no special software: Microsoft Office packages such as Excel will suffice. In very little time staff can produce useful portal solutions for various information needs.

Librarians have always been central to the creation of information gateways for users. In the analogue world, we would create guides to subjects, indexes and the like. The digital world offers up opportunities to enhance this role if we can move beyond the straightforward role of instructing and guiding users into the arena of creating digital content for them. By demystifying what can be seen as an overtly technical subject and grounding the topic in the area of core information skills, it is hoped that readers may be encouraged to experiment with introducing simple portals in their own services where they do not currently exist, or where provision is currently too broad to cover overtly specific information needs.

Portals in libraries and beyond

The more famous examples of portals are those well-used resources we tend to take for granted in the modern world – namely web search engines or directories such as Yahoo!

Certainly there are many commercial companies who have viewed portals as a way of attracting users to their site, the one-stop shop concept being the main marketing tool. Butters has expressed doubts that portals can be all things to all people, as he states:

It is likely that if a portal was to attempt to provide 'all things for all people' . . . there might be too much on one screen and too many channels to choose from. Thus no single portal is likely to serve all purposes. Different portals will require suitable sets of features as appropriate to the job in hand.   (Butters, 2003)

One of the main reasons libraries continue to be crucial to the information needs of their community is this inability of the large-scale portal to solve all needs.

An interesting development in the portal concept has been the move on the part of library management system (LMS) suppliers to enter into the market. This seems a logical progression, as web-based online public access catalogues (OPACs) have become the norm, it seem sensible to extend these by making them a part of a larger information screen that the user encounters when sitting themselves at a library terminal, or accessing the web OPAC from home. There remains the problem, however, of users mistaking such screens as a panacea for all of their information-seeking ills, and the development of such portals remains a challenge. As has been stated in the university library context:

The complexities of searching multiple sources including the library catalogue, multiple e-journal collection interfaces, and multiple bibliographic databases to find references and locate the full text, reflected in inefficient use of document delivery and ILL, has come to be seen as a critical problem for user education.

(Cox and Yeates, 2003, 155–6)

The public library could be argued to have even more of a challenge in terms of information literacy among its customers than many of the universities, making the design of such solutions all the more crucial if they are to be effective. While such solutions may be of more immediate use to the education sector, it is worth keeping an eye on and informing such developments as a matter of urgency. It is certainly the case that the purchase of an add-on module for an LMS that provides a portal solution for a public library could save an authority a considerable amount of time and money.

Some local authority organizations have implemented portal projects on their own for their particular information needs, in many cases with the input of library staff, and the growth of bespoke portals in the public sector has been great in the UK over the past few years. Perhaps the most well-known example of a portal solution undertaken in the public sector in the UK is the seamlessUK project:

The Seamless Project was funded by the British Library Research and Development Fund and established a Web-based, interactive, citizens' information service for the people of Essex. It provided a common interface to information in a variety of formats (Web pages, databases, Word documents) produced by 29 key information providers.

(Atherton, 2002, 468)

One of the key aspects of the project's success was its collaborative nature; it involved input from nine local authority partners in the south east of England, and focused on the creation of robust metadata standards. It set new standards for local authority e-services, allowing the user to search across many platforms for information. As well as the ability to access information from the local authorities involved, the user can also access government organizations, the BBC, and learning organizations such as learndirect. Other local authorities have been learning from the seamlessUK example, which as a project is an exemplar. With the user being central to the concept, the portal is designed to be especially straightforward to use:

It does not demand that the user has a lot of knowledge about search techniques, about local authority responsibilities and services or about geographical boundaries. Citizens can search for local information or national information in one easy search. Partnerships and co-operation make this possible. (Atherton, 2002, 468)

Removing the barrier that exists in the mind of many users about which organization to approach for a particular service is a positive move forward in information provision. Rather than being precious about the services each organization provides, the collaboration offers a one-stop shop that allows the service and not the organization to be central to the information-seeking of the user.

Other prominent portal projects will be discussed in the case studies below.

CASE STUDY

Building a website portal for the Greater Pollok community (www.greater pollok.net/)

Author: Margaret Houston, Digital Network Manager (Pollok)

The Greater Pollok area of Glasgow is in the south of the city. It is an area defined as a social inclusion partnership (SIP) area owing to its high levels of unemployment and other community needs. The goal to build a portal for the community was an ambitious one, as it was more than merely building a technical solution, but actively involving the community throughout the process, ensuring it met community needs. Funding was provided by the Scottish Executive, via Scottish Enterprise Glasgow, as part of a wider initiative, 'Greater Pollok: a connected neighbourhood'.

There were many challenges when the project began in the autumn of 2003. One of the first was deciding how the technical component of the project would be addressed. While there was a digital network manager (seconded from Glasgow City Council's Cultural and Leisure Services – a key partner in the connected neighbourhood initiative) responsible for the portal project, the work itself would be placed out to tender, since it involved a high level of interactivity and technical sophistication. The first step was to create a wish list of what the portal should do. This task involved looking at many current examples of community websites to identify features and elements that should be incorporated into the Greater Pollok model. However, the main goal for this initial search was to present the examples to the members of the community.

Community involvement in the process

A website design group (WDG) was formed to act as a discussion forum for the community to express their views on the project, and to make crucial decisions about the design and content. Strong community involvement (or 'buy in') from the beginning was deemed essential to the success of the project. The group was formed after a marketing campaign, which involved the digital network manager placing posters and leaflets in busy community venues, such as community centres, the local library, Cybercafé, and putting an article in the local newspaper. The response was extremely good, and meant the project had positive community involvement from the beginning. One of the key criteria for the group was to ensure it was representative of all strands of the community, therefore members were selected to reflect the diversity of the community, and included the young, the elderly and the disabled.

At the first meeting the digital network manager explained the concept of a community portal to the WDG. This was presented in a way that acknowledged the varying levels of ICT ability or knowledge present in the WDG. Using the analogy of the portal as a community magazine was effective and enabled members to visualize the end product. This seemed to work well, and ideas flowed from the less ICT literate members when they divorced the content element from the technical issues. It was considered vital that the final say on designs should rest with the digital network manager as any disagreements could hold up the design process. Fortunately, the consensus approach has worked well to date with all opinions considered and discussed thoroughly.

The first meeting of the WDG concentrated on presenting the examples of other community portals to the members for their consideration. The digital network manager described what a community portal is, and the types of content it could include, and sought views from the members as to their wishes for the resource. The group found this immensely informative, and critiqued the examples given in an extremely informative and constructive way. One of the more positive aspects of this critiquing exercise was the sense of ownership the group then began to feel for their own portal. The consensus being that the Greater Pollok portal would take all of the best elements of the critiqued examples and indeed improve on them. This was exactly the kind of community involvement hoped for at the beginning of the project.

Wider consultation on design issues

The successful company in the tender process to build the site next produced five design choices for the portal, based on the feedback from the WDG. The designs were produced in a web version and in hard copy, made available in ring binders and given to community activists who showed the designs to their peers and asked for comments. This approach widened the consultation process as community groups and other stakeholders who may not have access to the technologies were able them to view them. It was also arranged for the wider community to be able to view the designs by:

- placing the ring binders in key community access points; voting sheets were included for community to members to choose their favourite
- asking the local cybercafé to display boards with the designs and seek views from their patrons
- encouraging residents accessing the web to go online and view the designs, and vote for their favourite.

An overall favourite (with another design a close runner up), emerged from the five designs, and interestingly this design incorporated a mix of the services on offer in the examples we had chosen from other sites. In essence, a mix and match approach had emerged, which validated best practice in other site designs and brought them together into the Greater Pollok example.

Content and features

Some of the key features included in the design of the portal are listed below. The key priority was local content, information of direct interest to the target community with a links section to other relevant or useful websites.

- **'People' photographs** – Incorporating people photographs helps define the site as being community focused, and makes it feel accessible.
- **Forums and chat facilities** – It is important to let the local community have their say about their area and the issues involved. Notwithstanding the potential pitfalls in providing such avenues for online communication, properly administered, it can provide a useful democratizing element to such a portal. Passwords and administrators are essential; as well as being important for security, they should also help people take responsibility for what they say online.
- **Vote section** – this provides an opportunity for users to vote on issues relevant to their community and perhaps influence decision-makers about funding spend and so on. An example of a recent vote asked for community views on dealing with litter offenders. Something as simple as littering can have a demoralizing effect on a community, and voting on an issue can highlight the problem and sometimes enables solutions to be found. Local organizations, community groups and individuals are encouraged to suggest topics to vote on. As with every area of the site currency is vital. Refreshing the topics frequently is always important, as the ability to express a view may be the one reason someone visits the portal before they find other material to engage them, as their confidence with the site grows. It is also a good idea to archive past votes to allow them to be viewed.
- An up-to-date **News** section promotes local news and is updated frequently. The recruitment of a volunteer bank of web 'reporters' to provide content for this section can engage the community even more by making them a part of the news and information gathering process. A link on the News page connects to the local community newspaper on PDF format.
- **Competitions** – A monthly competition, with prizes, acts as an incentive for the community to return to the site again and again. Local businesses may wish to sponsors a competition by providing prizes in return for a credit mention on the site.
- An unusual feature of the Greater Pollok Portal is a **Celebrations** area, which allows users to submit their celebration photos, such as 100th birthdays, graduations, weddings and christenings. This encourages family and friends to visit

to view their celebration on the site – it is a digital version of a 'mention' on the radio!

- An interactive **Calendar** is prominently placed on the homepage and allows organizations to add their events. This popular feature ensures greater publicity for local events and potentially increased community participation, so promoting community cohesion. In the future the Calendar will link to information on how to book a place at the events featured, if appropriate.
- We have added an '**Introducing**' section where community activists and workers can introduce themselves – with photograph and brief details and an opportunity for them to get the key messages of their service across to the community.
- **Directory** – This lists all of the organizations in the area and gives them their own page with their details, address, purpose and the like. Users can then search for organizations, businesses and learning providers that interest them. Allowing the groups listed in the Directory to update their details on their own is a useful feature, although it may necessitate a high level of administration to begin with, and the issue of usernames and passwords. Local politicians should also be included to enable the portal to act as a conduit for the community to engage with their elected representatives. Short training sessions for groups and organizations wishing to appear on the Directory are then arranged, teaching them how to upload information themselves directly into the system, by means of a unique password.
- **Historical photographs and memories** of the area. The Greater Pollok Portal links directly into the Greater Pollok Kist website, which contains old photographs of Greater Pollok, and to the Mitchell Library's 'Virtual Mitchell' resource, which features old photographs of the Glasgow area. A future addition will be the ability to click on a photo and hear residents' memories; this could become part of a school project, where pupils will be involved in collecting the audio reminiscences as part of a larger project aimed at researching their local area.

While it is still early days for the portal, one of the key future developments will be the expansion of e-government aspects to the site. With the focus on digital citizenship, the portal can provide opportunities to inform and engage the community politically. Research will be conducted into the needs of the community in this area, and incorporated into additional functionality on the portal.

An interactive map is also being prepared, which when passed over with a mouse will link to new building projects that are planned to regenerate the

Greater Pollok area. The links could feature electronic building plans and information on any job opportunities – and application forms – that may arise from the developments. The community can therefore be kept well informed about the regeneration of their area.

CASE STUDY

The East Renfrewshire experience

Author: Liz McGettigan, Information Services Manager

East Renfrewshire Council has to date developed two successful portal projects, namely Barrhead-Scotland.com and the Holocaust Memorial Day site. Both examples, discussed below, illustrate the diversity of projects library staff can become involved in when using digital solutions to satisfy information needs within the communities they serve.

Barrhead-Scotland.Com

In 2000 the Bill and Melinda Gates Foundation made available finances to help fund community ICT initiatives. East Renfrewshire Council successfully bid to the fund to create a community portal for the Barrhead area of the authority.

The project aimed to promote inclusion and regeneration through the use of ICT. It focused on the development of a community website, acting as a one-door approach to information on Barrhead and its communities. Site content includes information on services, community agencies, voluntary groups, local businesses, leisure activities and events, and advice services, including health. The site also acts as a directory for local businesses, thus assisting in economic development.

The site is based around a community portal structure developed by the Cultural Services division of Community and Leisure, for the Council. Much of the site content is developed and created by the local community, and this is a key facet of the project. Teams of local residents, including young people, and those active within the community have been trained in the necessary skills to create web pages. This was done both in the community library and through outreach, using laptops. Volunteers were identified and supported through Voluntary Action, the local umbrella group for the voluntary sector.

Residents in Social Inclusion Partnership areas have been given opportunities to learn the skills required to access the site, through libraries, which concentrate on basic skills; Log-In, the internet café, which works with young people; and

Barrhead learning centre, which also supports progression to more formal qualifications. The project also enables residents who have no PC in the home to create and use their own e-mail address.

Our experience in developing learning centres and in building the site strongly
suggests that people need 'hooks' to motivate them to learn ICT skills, and to
access citizenship content. These hooks should relate strongly to people's own
lifestyles and experiences, providing them with a base from which they can
broaden out. By developing content on and with local communities, and by supporting access to that content, Barrhead.com has provided those hooks.

Part of the interactivity of the portal is built around themed forum areas, where
people can post on topics under seven categories:

- business
- community
- for sale
- general notices
- history and genealogy
- living in Barrhead
- young people.

We have found this to be a popular area of the site, where local residents can
communicate on topics as diverse as computer games to local history. The portal
has developed into a living and breathing resource for the community.

Holocaust Memorial Day (www.eastrenfrewshire.gov.uk/holocaust)

As the historic second city of the British Empire, Glasgow and its surrounding
area has seen much immigration in its history; and East Renfrewshire, just outside Glasgow, is home to the largest Jewish population in Scotland. As part of the
commitment to the ethnic diversity in the local community, the local authority
decided to build a community portal to commemorate Holocaust Memorial Day
in 2004, for which it was also hosting a commemorative exhibition. In creating
this website and exhibition we have developed content in line with national
Holocaust Memorial Day. The aim is to:

- recognize that the Holocaust was a tragically defining episode of the 20th
  century, a crisis for European civilization and a universal catastrophe for
  humanity

- provide a national mark of respect for all victims of Nazi persecution and demonstrate understanding with all those who still suffer its consequences
- raise awareness and understanding of the events of the Holocaust as a continuing issue of fundamental importance for all humanity
- ensure that the horrendous crimes, racism and victimization committed during the Holocaust are neither forgotten nor repeated, whether in Europe or elsewhere in the world
- restate the continuing need for vigilance in light of the troubling repetition of human tragedies in the world today
- reflect on recent atrocities that raise similar issues
- provide a national focus for educating subsequent generations about the Holocaust and the continued relevance of the lessons that are learnt from it
- provide an opportunity to examine our nation's past and learn for the future
- promote a democratic and tolerant society, free of the evils of prejudice, racism and other forms of bigotry
- support the government's commitment that all citizens – without distinction – should participate freely and fully in the economic, social and public life of the nation
- highlight the values of a tolerant and diverse society based upon the notions of universal dignity and equal rights and responsibilities for all its citizens
- assert a continuing commitment to oppose racism, anti-Semitism, victimization and genocide.

It was important to ensure our broad aims for the project were in line with those of the day. In this way the partnership developed could ensure we would create a resource that could achieve the broadest possible aims.

It was decided that the site would be developed with representatives from the Jewish community within East Renfrewshire and include unique audio testimonies, as well as links to a multitude of material on the Holocaust and genocide. Input was also sought from the disabled, homosexual and Romany communities to emphasize their barbaric treatment during the Holocaust, which is sometimes less well documented. One of the main goals for the site was to help ensure that the local community and especially young people would never forget the Holocaust and were also aware of current genocides. An accompanying CD-ROM would be created containing the same resources to help support wide dissemination of the project to schools and other community groups.

The emerging resource is built around five key sections:

- testimonies
- culture
- non-Jewish victims
- other Holocausts
- events and resources.

Building the portal under these headings was a huge undertaking, as it meant working with the community to gather resources. A vital component of the site would be the oral testimonies of members of the Jewish community in East Renfrewshire who had experienced at first hand the horrors of the Holocaust. It was felt this would bring the history to the young people in the community more realistically. Indeed, the origins and lives of the community are well documented via the oral testimonies, offering a glimpse of reality of what it was like being a Jewish person during the Holocaust. At the heart of the site would be the message of the universality of experience of victims of ethnic genocide. While the emphasis would be on the Jewish community, because of the nature of the day it was commemorating, the testimonials from other communities would put the experiences in a wider context for visitors.

It was important to the creators of the resource to allow young people to put the Holocaust in not only its World War 2 context, but as an example of how genocide can affect ethnic communities in the world across the decades. The site emphasizes other atrocities such as those seen in recent years in Cambodia, Rwanda and Bosnia-Herzegovina, which affected other ethic groups as well as the Jewish community. We involved the local schools in the area by involving them in creating artwork around the theme of Holocaust. This material is especially well suited to presentation via the site, and has ensured the site is a true community collaborative effort.

We have been immensely gratified by the feedback we have received since the exhibition opened and the site went live in January of 2004. A guest book on the site allows visitors to post their own comments about the information presented on the site and in the accompanying physical exhibition, which complemented the site. Below are some of the comments received about the exhibition, which we requested should be posted using the site:

07-JAN-04
I am proud that East Renfrewshire remembers the tragedy of the Holocaust every year, proud that we have the largest Jewish population in Scotland and proud that we have a large and growing Muslim population. I'm most proud

that we all live together as one community. Perhaps we are learning. If we are, a large part of the reason is this Memorial.

10-JAN-04

A moving and at times harrowing exhibition. I am so appreciative of the Council's expertise in putting on this display in conjunction with the other bodies concerned. I thought the venue, in such dignified surroundings, added to the poignancy of this event. I thought the way in which events in World War II were brought in to the context of present day life (Bosnia, Stephen Lawrence etc.) was especially relevant. Will we ever learn?

21-JAN-04

I learned a lot about what happened and I think it was a terrible thing. The more people who know about it the better and they should never be forgotten.

25-FEB-04

This is a brilliant website. Huge thanks to those who made this website possible, it's a great help for school projects. Cheers.

One of the most beneficial aspects to creating a web resource of an exhibition that may only be in a physical location for a short time is that the web version can remain available permanently, and to a larger audience of visitors from all around the country and the world. The Holocaust Memorial Day site, then, can stand as a testament for the future, and visitors to the site can access the gathered material 24 hours a day and 365 days a year, ensuring the hard work put into the development is continuingly worthwhile.

Libraries should be encouraged when creating local exhibitions for their community to create an electronic version simultaneously. When such a large amount of research is invested in providing an informative gateway to the information, it seems a wasted opportunity to allow the work to be limited only to a time when a physical exhibition can be sited.

Activities – Implementing simple portals for local information needs

In all of the examples cited above, there remains the core skillset that library staff have had as a central plank of their profession since it began: organization of information. While high-level portal solutions may provide library staff with solutions to a high proportion of their customers' information needs, and more bespoke ones, there remains a subset of ad hoc local needs that are in danger of being missed.

Although the discussion above has centred on larger-scale implementations of the portal concept in libraries, when no larger information solutions exist small-scale implementations are possible using easily available tools. Consider for instance the following information-seeking scenarios:

- A school pupil is interested in researching the Vikings. On further querying of the pupil you find out that this is part of a larger school project. You can thus expect many more queries on exactly the same topic, without enough book-based resources to provide a solution.
- A new resident in your local area is interested in finding more information on their new community. Their query encompasses various printed materials, and you know this type of information is all available electronically.

While such information is easily available via community information resources, it can also be easily available on the internet using a variety of sources, and in the modern age users are increasingly seeing the internet as the panacea for their information needs. One of the key roles of a community library should be to simplify the process of accessing this information on behalf of the user, and this can be done using the simplest of tools. As Rowley states, 'the process of the organization of knowledge involves three stages: selection and evaluation, organization, and re-selection or "weeding"' (Rowley, 2000, 221). The following suggestions for local solutions should consistently use this three-way process to ensure there are up-to-date information solutions. While being relatively simple examples of information organization, they illustrate easily constructed examples of the portal concept – namely providing a gateway to information on behalf of a user.

Activity 1 – A simple portal solution for school history projects

The scenario cited above, where a young user requested information on the Vikings for a school project, should be all too familiar to many community library staff in the UK; in the context of projects, one can substitute Victorians for Vikings, or Egyptians, or kings and queens – or many other topics. In many cases by the time the staff have had the time to figure out that many other young people will be asking the same question, most of the print-based resources have been issued to the first lucky borrower. With time being of the essence in these scenarios, there often is not enough time to obtain material from other libraries in the network.

The solution may then invariably be that the staff react to each enquiry as it comes in, spending much time duplicating the same answers to users and aiding them in finding further resources via the internet and other electronic-based materials. Some time spent in creating a resource base of materials for such enquiries can be time-consuming in the short term, but greatly valuable in the long term in enhancing staff skills, and enabling users to use previously evaluated and relevant material.

N.B. The following activities involve you using Microsoft Excel, and a web browser. For the purposes of the given examples, Microsoft Internet Explorer is used.

One of the continuous improvements to products such as Excel has been the ability to save data created in Hypertext Markup Language (HTML) format, the preferred method for viewing pages on the internet, and subsequently web browsers. One of the added benefits of this is that you can create a dataset, keep the original, and create an HTML copy for use by the public that ensures that the original dataset cannot be amended by accident or design.

The examples below offer a simple solution using software readily available in all libraries. Follow the steps below as an example:

Stage 1

Open Excel. At this stage you should already have given consideration to the headings you wish to use for organizing your information. If not, pause for a few moments to consider exactly how you may wish to retrieve the sources in the future. The example in Figure 6.1 gives an extremely simple organizational structure for the resources we will be entering, and is used as a starting point only:

	A	B	C
1	Topic	Location	Source
2			
3			
4			

Figure 6.1 Suggested headings for Activity 1

For the purposes of this example, we have chosen three headings: **Topic**, **Location** and **Source**. You may wish to have more categories; for instance instead of simply a **Topic** category, you may wish to use a **Subject** and a **Title** category instead. This activity will enable you to produce a simple set of resources and can be used to familiarize yourself with the software processes before you create a more detailed usable dataset.

Stage 2

Launch Internet Explorer. To begin creation of the resource base, we will search for material on Egypt relevant for school pupils. To this end we have already decided that we will use two main search engines:

- Kids Click (http://sunsite.berkeley.edu/KidsClick!/)
- Yahooligans (http://yahooligans.yahoo.com/)

For your own purposes, feel free to use any resources you feel appropriate. Remember, however, that the primary aim should be to provide good quality resources that are appropriate for the age group concerned. Both Yahooligans and Kids Click have excellent provenance, and you can be reassured that any resources they point you to have been previously evaluated as suitable.

Using Kids Click, enter the term 'Egypt' into the search box and click Search. When the search was undertaken for this chapter there were over 60 hits; 60 hits result in a lot of material for children to plough through, so you may decide at this point to have a quick look at the available links to choose the resources you feel might be the best.

Select a few of the resources to add in to the dataset, ensuring you enter the data in the following format:

1. SUBJECT – Website/Resource Title: 2. Location: 3. Source

Figure 6.2 shows how this will be presented.

	Topic	Location	Source
1	Topic	Location	Source
2	EGYPT -Ancient Egypt - A Sixth Grade Curriculum	http://www.angelfire.com/wi/egypt/index.html	Kids Click
3	EGYPT - The Great Sphinx	http://touregypt.net/sphinx.htm	Kids Click

Figure 6.2 Examples of how data can be entered

In the topic category, it is important that you enter the name of the website, after you have prefixed it with a subject heading, as the examples above suggest. As well as being good practice in terms of organization of information, it also aids the software when you get round to using the **Sort** facility at a later stage. Continue to enter resources you find useful.

After you have exhausted links on Kids Click, run the same search on Yahooligans and enter any new links you find of interest.

Tip: When entering the location or URL, you can greatly simplify the process by copying and pasting the link from the Address Bar of your browser into the cell. Pressing the Enter key once you have typed the address correctly will enable the location information as a web link.

Stage 3

After you are happy with the links you have gathered, it is time to turn the spreadsheet into a resource usable by the customers of the library. In its existing format, the data can be easily changed or reorganized by the user, either by accident or design. What we require is a solution that allows access to the resources, but does not allow any changes to the data or structure to be undertaken without authorization. A simple way of achieving this is to save the spreadsheet in the format of an HTML page. To do this, simply click File, Save As Webpage.

Give the new file you are creating a name, and click Save. As stated, this will create an HTML version of your dataset, which will be viewable in a web browser when clicked. Only issue this file to the customer, as full functionality will be available in terms of accessing the web resources; however, the customer will be unable to alter the data or reorganize it. Keep the master copy of the spreadsheet on a secure storage device, perhaps a disc or compact disc, or better still a staff-only computer or network drive. Being a digital object, multiple copies of the HTML page can easily be built up for use by more than one individual, perhaps class or school visits to the library for instance.

Extra activities

- build up multiple workbooks within one spreadsheet file and try to convert these into HTML resources. Talk to your young person's librarian in your service and ask for tips on good resources. Ask one library in your area to work on one subject, while you work on another – pool the data together when complete and share among the rest of the service.
- experiment with more detailed categories for organizing your data.

Activity 2 – Local community information via the web

A great benefit of the community library is its location in the heart of a geographic area. Community libraries can be one of the first places newcomers to an area visit for a quick snapshot of what's available. This is an information need community librarians have been meeting for decades, and with the increasing availability of electronic information, this need can be satisfied even more neatly than it has in the past.

Consider for one moment the power something as simple as a postcode has to enable people to find services and locate information on a specific geographic area. Many services offering access to information in this way have been introduced, perhaps the most famous being UpMyStreet.com (www.upmystreet.com/), which offers information on all aspects of modern life simply by entering a postcode, including maps. This kind of resource is extremely valuable for community libraries, and the next activity discusses how such services can be used.

The example below has been chosen at random by the authors, and without any prior knowledge of the area in question, to give an idea of how straightforward the activity can be. With your own personal knowledge of your community, you will be able to edit the material much more carefully. The area chosen is served by Birkenhead Central Library, postcode CH41 2XB.

Stage 1

Open Excel and create a simple spreadsheet with the following column headings:

Postcode   Services   Link   Source

Stage 2

Launch Internet Explorer and load up the home page for UpMyStreet.Com (www.upmystreet.com). In Internet Explorer, type in the following postcode to the search box: CH41 2XB. As previously mentioned, this is the postcode for Birkenhead Central Library. For the first activity, we will pretend we are interested in finding a list of primary schools in the area.

Click **Search** on the main page, and on the page that loads up immediately afterwards click the link that states, '**Find My Nearest**'. This will present you with a choice of categories for services in your chosen area. Click '**Education and Childcare**' and, on the following page, the category for '**Primary Schools**'. The next screen presents you with a list of primary schools in your chosen area, with distances in miles and yards from your point. Beside each school is also an option entitled '**Map**', which will allow you to view a map of each location.

It may seem quite a long-winded task to click through each option, but the important point to note is that the URL for the final search screen is a real link, which can be used at a later stage if saved. The link should read:

www.upmystreet.com/nrs/?l1=CH41+2XB&cat=1934

You can copy and paste this link into your Excel sheet and save it for future use. An interesting aspect to sites such as UpMyStreet is that the search query used by the user is visible in the final URL of the search. So for instance, in the URL above, the postcode can be clearly seen in the following format:

l1=CH41+2XB

While the extra information that relates to the primary school part of the search is located in the text that follows:

&cat=1934

Therefore, together, the search string states that we are querying the database for everything that is category 1934 in postcode CH41 2XB. Knowing this enables us to alter the postcode element of the URL and replace it with any valid postcode to rerun the search.

Stage 3

Copy the information from this search into your spreadsheet. For the purposes of this activity, under the Services column enter the subject as 'Education – Primary Schools'. In similar fashion to the last activity, if we now used the **Save As Web Page** option in Excel, we can produce a version of the spreadsheet in HTML format that will prevent the user from being able to tamper with the data.

Before doing that, however, run the same search for secondary schools, universities (under Further and Higher Education section), and pre-school groups, and enter them onto your spreadsheet. Figure 6.3 illustrates how your spreadsheet should look.

Consider some other topics you may like to look for; here are some suggestions:

Cinemas; Dentists; Hairdressers; Hospitals; Doctors

	A	B	C	D
1	Postcode	Services	Link	Source
2	CH41 2XB	Education - Primary Schools	http://www.upmystreet.com/nrs/?l1=CH41+2XB&cat=1934	Up My Street.com
3	CH41 2XB	Education - Pre-School	http://www.upmystreet.com/nrs/?l1=CH41+2XB&cat=1940	Up My Street.com
4	CH41 2XB	Education - Secondary Schools	http://www.upmystreet.com/nrs/?l1=CH41+2XB&cat=1937	Up My Street.com
5	CH41 2XB	Education - Universities	http://www.upmystreet.com/nrs/?l1=CH41+2XB&cat=1951	Up My Street.com

Figure 6.3 Postcode as community information locator

Your chosen topics are really as wide as those sourced by UpMyStreet. Take some time to add more data into your spreadsheet and, when you are happy, use the Save As Webpage option within Excel to create an HTML version that could be used by the customers of the library.

Conclusion

One of the key considerations for library staff has always been to put the correct information with the correct user. While large-scale portal solutions are becoming more common, in a community setting there remains a need for staff to engage in unique resource creation to enhance the services they provide for their customers. The activities above should give you a start in using pre-existing tools for this purpose, but it is important that staff continue to engage creatively with the tools at their disposal.

References

Arnold, K. (2001) Barriers to Access: intranet and internet portals, *Serials*, 14 (2), (July), 179–82.

Atherton, L. (2002) SeamlessUK – Building Bridges Between Information Islands, *Library Review*, **103** (1182/3), 467–73.

Butters, G. (2003) What Features in a Portal?, *Ariadne*, **35**, www.ariadne.ac.uk /issue35/butters/intro.html [accessed 17 February 2004].

CILIP (2002) *An Investment in Knowledge: library and information services in the United Kingdom*, London, CILIP.

Cox, A. and Yeates, R. (2003) Library Portal Solutions, *Aslib Proceedings*, **55** (3), 155–65.

Debowski, S. (2000) The Hidden User: providing an effective service to users of electronic information sources, *OCLC Systems & Services*, **16** (4), 175–80.

O'Leary, M. (2000) Grading the Library Portals, *Online*, **24** (6), (Nov/Dec), 38–44.

Pinto, F. and Fraser, M. (2003) Access Management, the Key to a Portal: the experience of the Subject Portals Project, *Ariadne*, **35**, www.ariadne.ac.uk/issue35/SPP/intro.html [accessed 17 February 2004].

Rowley, J. (2000) Knowledge Organization for a New Millennium: principles and processes, *Journal of Knowledge Management*, **4** (3), 217–23.

Zhou, J. (2003) A History of Web Portals and their Development in Libraries, *Information Technology and Libraries*, **22** (3), (September), 119–28.

7

Creating digitized content in community libraries

David McMenemy

Introduction

With the increase in access to ICTs in libraries, public library staff have been trained to understand how to best employ the technology for the benefit of the user. Yet there currently lies a relatively untapped world of information in community libraries across the United Kingdom. While there have been a myriad of projects aimed at digitizing content, they have predominantly been centrally managed and offered a piecemeal approach to the topic. This chapter, then, has four main aims:

- to discuss the importance of digitization in the context of community libraries
- to define file formats and popular software for digital conversion
- to highlight some examples of best practice
- to encourage community library staff to use available resources for creation of their own digital content to enhance their service to customers.

While the People's Network put in place the infrastructure in the UK's public libraries, and other initiatives such as NOF-Digitise and the Public Libraries Challenge Fund made inroads into content creation, there remains a dearth of local community content in digital format available for many users. Given that each community library across the country will have some kind of local history collection that contains some images or other visual materials, there is a great argument for community library staff to become involved in using this material in a digital environment. As Simon Tanner has stated:

> The role of librarians is changing and libraries are not just storehouses but promoters of information. Library and information professionals, as ever, need to be focused upon meeting their specific community's needs, and provide the expertise to guide their users through the ever burgeoning mass of electronic resources. This user perception of what is needed from a librarian is from a custodian to a friendly expert, guide, fundraiser, resource provider, creator and distributor of information. These user desires are a powerful driving force in our newly wired world. (Tanner, 2001, 327)

Therefore staff must become as comfortable in the promotion and exploitation of digital resources as they are in traditional formats, and one way of doing so is to enhance the use of the resources by using digital technologies.

The digital image can be used in many more ways than the paper original. For instance, the image can be inserted into a word-processed document, or a web page. It can be printed on a basic printer, or e-mailed to someone on the other side of the world. It can be enhanced with software, improving the image or completely destroying its original features. The digital image can be used as the centre-piece for a larger dissemination of the content it represents, for example in a web page or some kind of electronic or online exhibition. As will be seen in the suggested activities later in this chapter, the digital image in a community library setting can be used to initiate projects for customers where their understanding and appreciation of their local community can be greatly enhanced by engaging with enriched content.

What is digitization?

In its simplest definition, digitization is creating a digital copy of an analogue object. When we scan an image we take a physical form and transform it into an electronic file that is viewable with a computer. Whenever we surf the internet and view an image, we are viewing a digital image, a digital representation of something that was originally in the real world. There are many advantages to digitizing content, as Hughes notes: 'Digital content can be browsed easily, and can be searched, indexed or collated instantly. Most importantly, it can be linked to a whole "web" of other content, either locally or globally via the internet' (Hughes, 2004, 4).

Digital content is value-added, not merely in terms of the ability to store and manage the resource, but in terms of providing enhanced access to the user. There is also an increasing level of expectation from users that such material will be easily available to them. It is important, then, that staff serving their local community begin to use such technologies. There is a great deal of increased professional confidence that can be gained by becoming involved in creation of digital content, as well as the benefits to users of the service.

Types of digitization

The most obvious example of digitized content is the digital image. It is something we all encounter each day on the internet, or if we use a digital camera while on holiday or at a family event. When the images are uploaded to the computer for printing or processing, we are engaging with digital content in ways that were practically unheard of even ten years ago. Many of us now own mobile phones with the ability to capture digital images and instantly send them to friends via e-mail or multimedia messaging services (MMS).

This explosion in digital imaging has been as a direct result of the inexpensiveness of the available technology; a good scanner can be bought for around £300, with equipment that is completely acceptable for producing internet images available for under £40. If your community library owns a scanner, it is likely to be in the price range somewhere between these two. Understanding the types of digital images that exist, and the pros and cons of each, is absolutely necessary not merely for aiding the customer in using the scanners, but also for staff in creating their own digital content.

Sound can also be easily digitized these days, and the explosion in availability and use of MP3 files is obvious testament to that. As well as the straightforward conversion of audio recordings, something we always have to be aware of and try not to allow in community libraries due to copyright, voice can be saved directly onto any modern computer with a simple microphone. This opens up new avenues for combining image content with audio, and can be easily achieved. The activities discussed later in the chapter will give some hints at how to begin this.

Types of images – BMP, TIFF, JPEG, GIF and PNG

Note: Examples of all of the different types of images discussed below are available on the website that accompanies this book. When viewing the example images, consider subjects such as file size, image quality and time taken to download to your own computer, as these are the issues you need to consider when creating your own digital content.

The first part of this chapter covered digitization in general. This section discusses image formats and images from the point of view of scanning and digitization issues.

Most image formats use pixels per inch, sometimes referred to as dots per inch (ppi or dpi), as a quality benchmark when scanning. This refers literally to the number of pixels, short for picture elements, present in each inch of the image; the more pixels or dots, the better quality the final image will be. The ppi chosen when scanning is entirely subjective; for the web 75ppi is normally sufficient, while if you were scanning for preservation purposes you would be looking at a minimum of 300, and perhaps even 600. The ppi rate becomes important if a customer wishes to enlarge, or blow-up, an image for enhanced use. An image scanned at 75ppi would begin to pixilate very early on in the enlargement process – which means the image would begin to look blurred at the edges. This is because there is not enough definition in the original to allow it to be stretched in this way. It is important therefore to consider the use the digital image will be put to when deciding on the quality chosen in the scanning process. One thing to note is that file size increases exponentially the higher the ppi rate. Stuart Lee discusses a relatively straightforward formula for calculating file sizes in his excellent work on digital imaging (Lee, 2001).

The bitmap (BMP) file format is the standard file format supported by the Windows operating system. If, like most people when they first use a Windows-based computer, you have fooled around with using the Paint program, you will most likely have created a BMP file, as this is the default extension any image will be saved in when using this software. BMP files are normally large in terms of their file sizes. They are also not particularly good for archival purposes or for publishing, as they tend not be as vibrant to look at as formats such as TIFF or JPEG.

The Tagged Image File Format (TIFF) is the format of choice for the publishing industry and for archival purposes; indeed most digitization projects would choose the TIFF as the first file format they would use to transfer their analogue content into, and indeed create new digital images in. The TIFF format normally results in extremely large file sizes, and is rarely used for delivery of images on the internet. Many projects, while beginning with a TIFF file, create copies of the TIFF in JPEG format for delivery over the internet.

The JPEG is the most common file format associated with images, and is sometimes referred to as JPG, JPE or JFIF in its file suffix. The term JPEG is an acronym for Joint Photographic Experts Group. The JPEG format itself is extremely popular mainly because it allows images to be delivered in small file sizes, while maintaining much of the original quality on screen or in print. An important point to note, however, is that the JPEG image is what is known as a *lossy* format; this means that, while the file size can be kept extremely small, even when saved at the highest possible quality level, the file loses some of its original integrity. This renders it a bad choice if the ultimate goal of the digitization is preservation surrogacy.

The term *preservation surrogacy* is based around the debate on whether the digital image in any format can justifiably be deemed to be an appropriate surrogate copy of an analogue original. Edwards and Matthews define preservation surrogacy as, 'a copy that is offered to the user in lieu of the original, normally to protect the original' (Edwards and Matthews, 2000, 140). The main arguments against the digital image being deemed an apt surrogate for the original centre around the transient nature of computer file formats. While the nature of digital files should certainly remain constant for the foreseeable future, being made up of the standard binary format of a series of 1s and 0s, image file formats are dependent on specific software and hardware solutions to view. An original photograph can be easily viewed by opening the album or simply placing the image on a surface, or holding it in your hand. The digital image, on the other hand, requires a digital delivery solution.

The Graphics Interchange Format (GIF) was the image format of choice in the early days of the internet, before JPEGs. GIFs are especially good for logos and the like, and you often will still see the format on websites for this reason. A GIF image can be either:

- interlaced – when downloading the image appears to dissolve into shape
- animated – a series of images have been combined into one file to give the appearance of animation
- transparent – a specific colour on the image is invisible; this often results in a light background completely disappearing and the foreground image appearing to be part of the fabric of a web page.

It is unlikely you will ever scan a photograph into this format for the reason that the viewing quality is nowhere near as good as that of the JPEG or TIFF. Compare the example of the GIF image on the book's website with that of the JPEG. There is a distinct difference in the quality of the viewed image. Again, however, like JPEG files, another benefit of the GIF is that file sizes tend to be small.

The final file format is the portable network graphics (PNG) format. This format, rather than using pixels to make up its structure, uses geometric shapes. It is growing in popularity and is especially prominent in plug-ins such as Macro-media Flash.

The main point to note in the discussion of these file formats is the difference in size versus the difference in viewing quality. Figure 7.1 illustrates the difference in file size of the exact same image saved in the five file formats discussed. As you can see, the BMP version of the image is almost 40 times the size of the JPEG version, yet there is little discernible difference to the viewer.

Name	Size ▼	Type
background.bmp	2,344 KB	Bitmap Image
background.TIF	1,818 KB	Microsoft Office Do...
background.PNG	1,041 KB	PNG Image
background.GIF	330 KB	GIF Image
background.JPG	60 KB	JPEG Image

Figure 7.1 Image format and file sizes

This is not really an issue when viewing an image file on your own computer, except perhaps in terms of storage space. However imagine if you are attempting to download ten images of the same size as the BMP file at the same time. There is little trade-off in viewing quality, for all of the benefits of speed of access and many more files to the available storage space when using the JPEG format.

Software for image creation

Software for manipulating and saving the digital image is absolutely essential. While you may receive various different brands of software depending on the scanner package you purchase, they all have similar goals; that is they enable you to manipulate an image, and save it in various formats. The Microsoft Office package itself contains a program called Photo Editor, which you can use to scan and save images. The aforementioned Paint program, which is a standard on Windows systems, can be similarly used. Other more expensive solutions exist, programs such as Adobe Photoshop allow sophisticated manipulation of digital images, and are standards in the media and advertising industries. However, for the standard user the key skill to learn is how to transform an image from one file format into another. It is likely that most readers will have a copy of Photo Editor at their disposal, and this can be used easily to achieve excellent results.

Luckily the majority of file types created by imaging software are readable across different imaging packages; certainly TIFF, BMP, JPEG and GIF files can be read by a standard internet browser like Netscape Navigator or Internet Explorer and most of the currently available software packages. This universality means that you can be assured creation of a digital image does not necessitate viewing of the image using the same package you used to create the file.

Storage of scanned images

Much of this chapter assumes that you will be wishing to store any digitized images as well as use the image for creating enhanced content, though for some of the activities discussed later in the chapter this is not absolutely necessary. One of the biggest concerns after scanning an item is where to store the master file. When scanning images file sizes can be extremely large, certainly greatly in excess of floppy disk size in a format like TIFF or BMP. When deciding to scan to create high quality surrogates of the original, then, it is essential to do so using a computer that has either:

- a connection to a network drive where images can be permanently stored
- a removable media device such as a zip drive or other external hard drive
- a CD or DVD burner.

When working with images, even large hard drives can become filled quickly, so a permanent solution needs to be devised if the purpose of the project is to store master copies. Even transferring images from one computer to another can be problematic if the file size is excessive. For use in projects involving working with members of the public a useful solution may be to purchase some USB pen drives. These are small devices which can hold up to 1GB of memory and can be taken from computer to computer with relative ease. They are extremely portable and convenient, and cost as little as £30 a device.

Perhaps, for instance, a solution to the larger problem of storage may be to save any master copies on CD-ROM and store them in a central point for the entire library service, all CDs being sent to one storage depot to ensure a central collection exists. This is certainly worth thinking about as a solution to the issue of storage, as it ensures an archival aspect to the project while also allowing the community library access to the images to promote and enhance for other projects. The choice is entirely subjective; however, it is wise to consider these issues before you begin any scanning programme, and if the decisions can be made on a service-wide basis rather than merely a local one, that is all the better.

The challenge of indexing the digital image

You may already have a database or card catalogue of your image collections, and the simplest way of creating a digital record of your images would be to use this pre-existing source. Even if you do, you may find the records for each image are insufficient for the needs of retrieval. One of the challenges of the digital age is that indexing has become eminently more complex; users expect to be able to find sources under many more categories than they perhaps did in the past. An excellent example of how complex the indexing of images can become can be seen on the Corbis image database (www.corbis.com). Run a search on the term 'dog' on the site, and you will certainly be faced with a huge number of hits. However, click on any one of the hits to view the larger version, scroll down and see the keyword categories they have indexed the image under. On the day we performed this simple search we clicked on the image of a Scottie dog titled 'Terrier on Grass', which was a relatively straightforward image of a dog in a field. It was found that the image was keyword indexed under terms such as:

- animals
- carnivores
- cute
- nobody
- harnesses
- restraints
- two-dimensional works.

These were only some of the terms used to index the image. As a commercial image bank, Corbis needs to attempt the widest dissemination of all of its images, however their indexing policy does illustrate the difficulties of meeting the expectations of users when retrieving images. Users need to be able to find an image before they can even begin to use it. As has been stated, 'A valuable resource is only valuable if those who need it can find it' (Nicholson and MacGregor, 2003, 98).

Activity 1

Spend some time surfing the Corbis site and try to imagine how you would have indexed some of these images. Check to see if the site has any images of local interest to your users. Would you have indexed these images in the same way?

Digitization projects in the UK

There has been a massive growth in the UK in digitization projects over the past five years. While many started in a local setting, there has also been a massive investment in local projects from the same source that invested so heavily in the People's Network programme, namely the New Opportunities Fund (NOF). It is apt that the focus on infrastructure and content creation were seen as equally important, as the network that existed needed content that was of interest to the population who would be using the new computer terminals. The aim of the NOF-Digitise programme was: 'to create innovative online resources of benefit to every UK citizen, bringing together over 500 partner organisations to create support for lifelong learning under the broad themes of citizenship, re-skilling, and cultural enrichment' (Nicholson and MacGregor, 2003, 96). The £50 million investment has led to the creation of a portal where users can access all projects funded under the initiative, Enrich UK (www.enrichuk.net/).

The Enrich UK portal gives some indication of the various types of content that have been digitized under the NOF programme. Accessing the site and clicking the browse option offers the opportunity of exploring the contents of the site. What is instantly evident is the range of material available in terms of coverage. Browsing under the topics of 'Our Past' and 'Local History', for instance, reveals projects on such diverse topics as the archives of the Old Bailey in London, the Staffordshire Past Track Digital Archive, and the British Pathe News archive. Sites like Enrich UK offer some excellent examples of best practice if you are thinking of producing your own digital content. For instance, look at as many sites as you can manage and think critically about issues such as:

- how the images are used to enhance textual content (and vice versa)
- whether you are able to click on smaller thumbnail copies of images to produce larger versions
- whether the content is appealing enough and the sites attractive enough to attract users.

There is certainly a challenge when choosing which materials to digitize, the danger being you could choose material that is particularly liked by you or other staff members rather than material that would be popular with customers (McMenemy and Shah, 2001, 33). An excellent example of how the balance between educational material and popular material has been struck is in the American Memory site at the Library of Congress (http://memory.loc.gov/). At this site you can view content as diverse as historic baseball cards and adverts for

Coca-Cola, to unique material on the history of African Americans and historical images of the American Civil War. The trade-off between popular content and content that might be deemed to be educationally important is an important one to strike in a digitization project if support from all stakeholders in the community is to be gleaned. In the community library context, content once digitized needs to be promoted and developed to enable customers to engage with the value-added nature of the medium.

Activity 2

Explore the content databases provided by EnrichUK and American Memory. How easy do you find them to search? Do you notice anything regarding the differing types of content they provide for their users?

An example of a project funded under the Scottish Office Challenge Fund is the Virtual Mitchell project (www.mitchelllibrary.org/vm). Sited at Glasgow City Council's famous Mitchell Library, the project aimed to make available online 10,000 images from the collections of the Mitchell Library and Glasgow City Archives (McMenemy and Shah, 2001, 33). An interesting aspect to the project was the community-driven focus; as well as scanning material that was housed in the collections of the library, residents in the city were encouraged to bring their own images to their local library to be added to the collection. This reflects a vitally important point, namely that much unique local historical content lies out with the ownership of libraries. How many people in the local community, for example, have in their photograph albums images of historical importance? This is an issue that community librarians could make a core part of their own digitization initiative, encouraging local community members to bring in their own photographs to be scanned and returned by library staff. The potential to enhance the local history collection of the library is an obvious benefit, but so too is the increased potential of engaging with the community in building a seamless resource.

An interesting point to note about the delivery solution chosen for the Virtual Mitchell project is its approach to presenting the digital images to the user. The project chose to use a commercial system for delivery of the materials, which has been a common solution for many digitization projects. One of the advantages of such a system is the sophistication it can produce in terms of delivering images in various sizes for differing purposes. The first stage in the search results produces a screen of thumbnail images, normally nine to a screen, with basic captions on the content. Clicking on any one of these thumbnails produces a more detailed view of the picture, with enhanced information on the image. Clicking on this enhanced image produces a full-screen version of the image that can be properly viewed. Such delivery solutions can be expensive, and many are available off-the-shelf for large fees, but the basic principle is a good one and can be incorporated into home made solutions as well as commercial ones.

Creating simple digital content

As discussed above, there are many reasons why digitization is something community library staff should be involved in as a core service for their customers. After all, who is better placed to understand local content and local issues than the staff who serve that specific community? Some of the main reasons for creating digitized content in community libraries include:

- to increase user access to the resources held by the library
- to preserve an original (because only the scanned version need be accessed by the public for most uses)
- to enable the content to be used more creatively by both staff and users.

All of these benefits can be easily achieved by virtue of a simple scanner, and some time and effort.

Activity 3 – Scanning images

There is no substitute for experience using a scanner. While not a complex task in itself, scanning an image is something that takes practice to do well. The information covered in Chapter 1 and earlier on in this chapter detailing file formats is vital to understand while undertaking this exercise.

- Choose the images you are planning to scan. Create a directory called 'Image Samples' on your desktop, or another easy-to-access part of your computer.
- Scan one of the images at 300dpi/ppi as a colour TIFF file. How long does this action take? What is the resultant file size?
- Re-scan the same image as a grayscale file in the same format. Is there any difference in file size?
- Using the Save As option in your imaging software, save a copy of the first scanned file as a JPEG file into the same directory. What difference do you notice in file sizes now?

- Try the same for other images. Try to vary between colour and grayscale images. Try scanning in different formats until you feel comfortable with what each format represents in terms of quality and file size. Alter the dpi rate and consider the difference this makes in terms of file size, and the time taken to scan the image.

Activity 4 – Creating a database of images for public use

Once you have scanned some images, the next challenge is to place them in some type of searchable delivery mechanism to be accessed by users. Again, most readers will have access to software that will enable them to create a simple delivery system. You can choose to create a database in Access, or use Excel to create the data source. This example will talk you through creating some simple records in Excel, and creating an HTML version of the index. You may already have a pre-existing index system to the images you are choosing, and you can choose to use this data for your image database, or augment it at the time with extra indexing terms if you choose to do so.

To avoid copyright problems, we are using images in this example taken with a digital camera on a holiday in Arran in the summer of 2003. The indexing terms used then, refer to the specifics of these pictures.

- Download the example images for this exercise from the website accompanying this book. There are only seven in total and all are of small file size. Ensure you save them in a folder called 'Images' and save that folder in the same directory that you save the example Excel files we will be building in this exercise.
- Open Excel and create a new spreadsheet with the following column headings:

Location	Description	Date	Keywords	Image

Enter the data as listed in Figure 7.2.

1	Location	Description	Date	Keywords
2	Arran	Brodick Castle - ancient home of the Duke of Hamilton	1 July 2003	Arran; Scottish Island; Scotland; castle;

Figure 7.2 Index entry for image database

You will notice that we have not entered anything into the 'Image' column as of yet. What we will do in this column is place a hyperlink to the particular image that this data entry represents. To do this, click on the Hyperlink button at the top of the screen, or click Insert, Hyperlink, while highlighting the appropriate cell. This will present you with a screen allowing you to select the file you wish to Hyperlink to. If you have saved the Images folder you previously downloaded into the same folder as you are working from, you should see this folder straight away. Double-click on the folder and highlight the appropriate image, in this case the file name is 'Image(35).jpg'. You will see that a blue hyperlink will appear, which when clicked on will display the image.

- Complete the data entry shown in Figure 7.3; or if you feel like you have time, add more keywords, or alter the descriptions of the images as you please.
- Saving the spreadsheet as a web page at this stage will create an HTML file viewable using a web browser. Clicking on the image hyperlink in this file will open the image in the web browser itself. Save the spreadsheet as a web page, and try out the new resource you have created.
- Try creating a similar resource for some of your own images. Try to think about appropriate categories for your initial spreadsheet. For instance, a database of local images may necessitate column headings such as postcodes, or local authority ward numbers, to ensure the images are findable under these unique terms.
- You could also try at this stage to import the spreadsheet data into a Microsoft Access database. This is relatively straightforward and is done by creating a blank database, then following the prompts from File, Get External Data, Import. At the next screen, select Excel spreadsheets as the file type, and if you have created the database file in the same folder as your spreadsheet, it should be instantly viewable. There are obvious benefits in having an Access version of your database, in terms of querying and the like. Importing the data from the Excel spreadsheet also gets over the cumbersome task of designing the initial database.

Location	Description	Date	Keywords	Image
Arran	Brodick Castle - ancient home of the Duke of Hamilton	1 July 2003	Arran; castle	Images\Image(35).jpg
Arran	A seagull eating a patron's lunch in Lamlash, Arran	1 July 2003	Seagull; Arran; sea	Images\Image(42).jpg
Arran	View of the sea from Corrie, Arran	1 July 2003	Sea; Arran	Images\Image(38).jpg
Arran	The ferry arriving at Brodick Pier, from a distance	1 July 2003	Ferry; Sea; Arran	Images\Image(36).jpg
Arran	A seagull eating a patron's lunch in Lamlash, Arran	1 July 2003	Seagull; Arran; sea	Images\Image(41).jpg
Arran	David's Mountain Bike	1 July 2003	Bicycle	Images\Image(40).jpg
Arran	David's Mountain Bike lying by edge of the sea	1 July 2003	Bicycle; Sea	Images\Image(39).jpg

Figure 7.3 Example index entries for the example images

Activity 5 – A simple multimedia local history project

As well as creating indexes to make your digitized content viewable, it is also a relatively straightforward activity to enhance the material by creating small multimedia projects built around the content. For instance, if you have a collection of digitized images, you could select some of them to create a small local history project that enhanced the images via audio content. Here are some more examples of how this technology can be used:

- Create a project working with children and the senior citizens in your community reminiscing about the history of the area. Older members of the community can be interviewed by the children and the audio can be merged with the images to create a testimonial of the community's history.
- A local anniversary or special occasion coming up? Use some images and record some audio to create an electronic exhibition to commemorate. You can loop the PowerPoint file to enable it to run constantly, where appropriate, for a set period of time.
- You could create a guide to the library services for new customers, giving audio instructions on how to use the catalogue, the rules and regulations regarding registering for internet access or membership of the library. Perhaps the file could be sent to local community groups, to encourage them to join the library.

As well as its other strengths, the PC is also an extremely efficient sound recorder, and using a microphone you can record audio as simply as you type and save a word processed file. To illustrate how easy it can be to make your images come alive, using the same images we used for the activity above, we will now create a multimedia presentation based on the content. To do this you will require the following additional resources:

- a microphone
- data presentation software such as Microsoft PowerPoint.

PowerPoint should be available as part of your Microsoft Office package, and any PC you have in the library that uses a webcam should also have a microphone you can use. If not, microphones and headphone sets can be purchased for around £10.

- *Step 1* – Open up PowerPoint and begin with a blank presentation template. On the title slide, enter the title 'Hungry seagulls and mountain bikes – a short trip to Arran'. Insert 'Image(38).jpg' from the downloaded images. For added effect, you can also insert some ocean sounds as background. To get these, click Insert, Movies and Sounds, Sounds from Clip Organizer. Then click on Clips Online and run a search on the resultant website for some sounds of the sea. Download these sounds to your computer, and insert the resultant clip.

- *Step 2* – Open the Sound Recorder and begin to record some voiceover for your slide using the text below:

'Welcome to some snapshots from a trip to Arran.'

Save the file you created as 'intro.wav' in the directory with your PowerPoint file. To add your own voice to the PowerPoint file, click Insert, Movies and Sounds, Sound from file.

- *Step 3* – Insert a new slide and call it, 'Ferry to Arran'. Insert 'Image(36).jpg' to illustrate the slide. Repeat the process above for recording some voiceover using the following text:

'The Ardrossan to Brodick Ferry is a very peaceful trip. And let's just say the chips are the best!'

Save the file you created as 'ferry.wav.' and insert it into the PowerPoint file.

- *Step 4* – Repeat the process for slides using any of the other pictures you wish to, and add your own commentary using the sound recorder. You can see how we approached this by downloading the 'Example presentation.ppt' file from the website supporting the book.

Experiment with these techniques to create multimedia presentations. The more confident you get using animation within PowerPoint, the more adventurous you can become. It is possible, for instance, to create interactive story times with PowerPoint using clip art and other images. Try downloading material from the Clips Online site to enhance your own work.

Conclusion

The creation of digital content should not be seen as solely the reserve area of staff involved in preservation areas. By creatively using the existing resources they have available, library staff can enhance how their users interact with the content. Simple tools like scanners and microphones can be used to improve the experience of the customer, and by involving the community in projects relating to their own local area, there is a great opportunity for the public library to become even more crucial to the lifelong learning needs of its clientele, as well as marketing itself to new audiences. As Hughes has stated, 'digital initiatives are a wonderful advertisement for the institution, and may increase requests from users to see the analogue resources' (Hughes, 2004, 28). Perhaps that previously underused local image collection could become a popular resource for the community.

For those readers who are interested in learning more about digitization, two books are worth obtaining for further reading. *Digital Imaging: a practical handbook* (Lee, 2001), explains in great detail how to understand and manage the scanning process, while *Digitizing Collections: strategic issues for the information manager* (Hughes, 2004), discusses all aspects of project managing a digitization project. Both are highly recommended for library staff wishing to gain further knowledge of the digitization concept.

References

Edwards, A. and Matthews, G. (2000) Preservation Surrogacy and Collection Management, *Collection Building*, **19** (4), 140–50.

Gallimore, A. (1999) Managing the Networked Library, *Library Management*, **20** (7), 384–92.

Hughes, L. M. (2004) *Digitizing Collections: strategic issues for the information manager*, London, Facet Publishing.

Lee, S. D. (2001) *Digital Imaging: a practical handbook*, London, Library Association Publishing.

Library and Information Commission (1998) *Virtually New: creating the digital collection*, London, LTC.

McMenemy, D. and Shah, A. (2001) From Tea to ICT, *Library Association Record*, **103** (1), (January), 32–3.

Nicholson, D. and MacGregor, G. (2003) 'NOF-Digi': putting UK culture online, *OCLC Systems & Services*, **19** (3), 96–9.

Tanner, S. (2001) Librarians in the Digital Age: planning digitisation projects, *Program*, **35** (4), (October), 327–37.

Conclusion – towards a digital future

Delivering digital services is about skills, confidence, and a strong service ethic. This is something public libraries and public librarians have. Yet it would be naïve and misleading not to admit that these services bring fresh challenges. Staff need to learn new skills to sit alongside old skills; they need to play the part of teachers, gatekeepers, and content creators. All roles are as vital as each other in the digital future, and all are achievable goals.

With the new technologies will arrive new users – this is unquestionable. As has been observed in the context of Danish public libraries:

> New user groups with different norms and expectations will become users. They bring different patterns of behaviour with them. It will be a demanding task for staff to solve these problems. Public libraries also have to change the way of defining a collection in relation to access to information. It looks as though we have taken the first step into a future in which fundamental changes in the library setting will occur. (Pors, 2001, 309)

Yet this is a change public libraries should not fear. Just as traditional users can be marketed new digital services, so digital users can be marketed traditional services; it is open season for public librarians wishing to make users aware of everything their service has to offer.

Traditional vs modern?

It is hoped that those reading this book will have been reminded that technology is not the enemy of public libraries. As one of the last sectors in library and information work to face the convergence of information and computers into that new concept known as ICT it may seem that technology is transforming what has always been a rather traditional service. This is true, but transformation is a good thing, progress is important, relevance is vital for a successful public library service. In the UK, the People's Network has been an unprecedented experiment in world library circles. The investment it has placed in the public sector needs to be embraced and built on for the future.

In closing, and we hope not controversially, we argue that ICTs are just as important in modern public libraries as books are. Many traditional users (and traditional librarians!) may disagree with this concept and feel that it devalues the role of the book. It does not. The librarian's role is now and has always been to provide access to information in all of its formats, without discrimination, fear or favour. To do so in the 21st-century public library entails knowledge of ICT unheard of even five years ago. The new technologies in public libraries open up new worlds of possibilities for expanding the experiences of all users, traditional and new.

The traditional ethos of public libraries is alive and well in the UK, and it is thriving. As Hendry has stated:

> If public library professionals remember the reasons they came into this calling in the first place, and if that depleted spring of idealism and the ethos of public service can be tapped again, public libraries can once again be a force for social good and decency in society, as gatekeepers to the ICT revolution, and as mentors and teachers. Education and ICT give public libraries the opportunity to thrive and to contribute to a more decent inclusive society. Idealism and a sense of their own history is a special gift public librarians still possess. The profession should be among the custodians and propagators not of information but of the gift of reason: a gift that can turn information into knowledge, and then to understanding, reason and tolerance, and perhaps even a wee bit of wisdom; then we might achieve a just society. That is the role of public libraries in social inclusion.
> (Hendry, 2000, 447)

ICT offers an opportunity for public libraries to grow and become even more relevant to society and to the country. As a profession, public librarians should move into the digital future with confidence and pride – they will, after all, be at the forefront of the digital future.

References

Hendry, J. D. (2000) Past Neglect and Future Promise: the condition of UK public libraries now and over the last 20 years, *Library Review*, **49** (9), 442–7.

Pors, N. O. (2001) Misbehaviour in the Public Library: internet use, filters and difficult people, *New Library World*, **102** (1168), 309–13.

Index